Mind Over Marathon

Overcoming Mental Barriers in the Race of Life

Gabe Cox

Mind Over Marathon

Overcoming Mental Barriers in the Race of Life

www.RedHotMindset.com

First Printing: (September/2019)

Author: Gabe Cox

Endorsements For Mind Over Marathon:

"For many people, running is more than a form of exercise or a sport; it's also a vehicle for personal and spiritual growth. *Mind Over Marathon* is an inspiring and practical guide to this rich dimension of the running experience."

-- Matt Fitzgerald, Author of Life is a Marathon

"Gabe Cox offers valuable lessons and a compelling story that I couldn't put down. Well worth your time!"

-- Gillian Perkins, bestselling author, speaker, and entrepreneur

"Faith, unshakable self-worth, discipline, mindset — Gabe Cox sets the pillars of achievement deep into the bedrock of daily practice. Framed in the story of qualifying for the Boston Marathon, *Mind Over Marathon* is not only for runners, but for anyone who needs a boost to reach their highest purpose."

-- Kitty Turner, Founder and CEO of Daily House Publishing

"Gabe Cox has not only provided me with faith-based practical advice on how to live a life worth living. By sharing what it took to qualify for the Boston Marathon against all odds, she's provided a roadmap for readers to achieving their biggest dreams. What I love most about *Mind Over Marathon* is that it has given me permission to dream—something I've struggled with before. If you've ever wanted to dream big or have a dream that seems unattainable, I highly recommend this book."

-- Corrine Casanova, Publisher, Daily House

"I just wish everyone could have the experience of setting a goal that was really honestly out of reach, working so long until you grow into the person who can achieve that goal, and then actually live it out. It's amazing!"

-- Kristen Genet, 2019 Boston Marathon qualifier

Gabe Cox is a woman of excellence in mind, body, and spirit. Her excellence in mind is portrayed clearly, as she perseveres through adversity while striving to become the woman she feels led to become. Her process of becoming a woman of excellence is mirrored in her book. The success principles she learns while striving to become a marathon runner can translate into any person's life who chooses to also pursue excellence and increase their personal performance. The book is enjoyable and easy to read. Gabe's ability to communicate is a true gift, as are her personal convictions to her readers.

-- Alana Grotewold, CEO Grotewold International

Dedication

This book is dedicated to you, the reader, in hopes that it inspires you to dream a dream that seems out of reach and to go after it with all of your heart. When you look back on your journey, you'll realize you're a whole new person. I believe in you, and I know it's your time!

You are a winner. Just run YOUR race!!

Contents

Foreword

I am honored to have the role of introducing Gabe's very first book. I can't imagine a better person to write about pursuing your dreams and making them happen!

I first met Gabe at a certification training with other running coaches. My first impression was amazement that such a big personality and strong leader fit in such a small body! I was thrilled to find out this upbeat, friendly individual was coaching for my company, Moms on the Run. She seemed the perfect role model for our mission of inspiring women to reach their goals through fitness, fun, and friendship.

We would next cross paths when she was the winner of the very first race I ever put on. Who was this girl whose smile made it look so effortless? Soon after, I hired her to fill a temporary position, where I got to experience her can-do attitude firsthand. Gabe puts her whole self into everything she does. Sets a goal and makes it happen, and now, she is sharing her wisdom through her writing and her life coaching business.

Running is a physical sport most would say. We move our legs faster to bring up our heart rate and teach our lungs to do the job. We power up hills to build strength in our lower body and we increase our workouts to be longer and longer to improve muscular endurance. We remove physical barriers by training our bodies for the task.

There's another side of preparedness for sport that doesn't often get as much attention: mental training. Our minds control everything about our choices for our bodies, yet they get so little support to improve how they do the job. Runners will truly benefit from the techniques Gabe shares to replace doubts and fears with confidence and skills.

In the season of finishing her book, Gabe demonstrated these skills firsthand. Her training was halted by a slip on the ice during a winter run. It was inspiring to observe the way her mental preparation and positive attitude framed her experience of a serious injury, one that would keep her away from her favorite sport for at least half a year.

"I guess this will be a gift for me to slow down and enjoy the little moments." What other *RUNNER* uses those words the very first time she shares with the world that she has broken her ankle?

This inspiration was only the beginning of a series of social posts where Gabe would share with the world her journey of heartbreak, lifestyle change, and a long road to recovery, all without complaining.

Gabe had recently accomplished one of the most prestigious achievements a runner can come by, qualification for the Boston Marathon. Gabe's training was so integral to who she was. One doesn't think of Gabe and not imagine her running. (I just tried to picture her standing still. Nope! Can't do it.)

Yet here she was, unable to put weight on one leg and being told she would not run for at least 6 months. She was entitled to be frustrated. People certainly would have understood if she was angry; forgiven her for a few complaints. Instead, during this time she was an inspiration to everyone around her. Day after day she spread a positive message through her hardship. I watched in amazement as she continued to exemplify "mind over matter" in a way I just hadn't seen before.

Although runners will find an immediate connection to her story, this book is not just for runners. Life is filled with everyday challenges that we don't always have the tools to deal with. Gabe provides these tools. Regardless of the types of dreams you have for yourself, you will find the inspiration you need and the practical steps to take to set goals, train your brain to think about them in the right way, and work your plan to create a new reality.

You will come to understand how your mental training can change your performance in sport and in your life. You will discover how to create clarity and eliminate confusion in your vision for the future.

If you are a person of faith, you will appreciate the short devotionals that help you dig a little deeper. You will enjoy a sense of how much your dreams are in line with your calling to fulfill God's purposes for your life. If this doesn't describe you, you will still be inspired to dream again; to find greater meaning that will enrich every day.

I welcome you today to pursue your passion- even if you don't yet know what that is, I bet you will by the time you're done with this book!

Happy Dreaming,

Karissa Johnson

Founder & CEO, Moms on the Run

www.momsontherun.com

Introduction

Life is like a marathon, not a sprint. It's an endurance race. It takes time, training, emotional stability, consistency, discipline, and so much more. Whether you're competing in an actual race or navigating the marathon of life, learning the keys to developing a positive mental attitude is vital for success.

Even though I relate success principles to running, everything that I have laid out in this book can be applied to any area of your life. I have added a reflection at the end of each chapter with a devotional, thought-provoking questions, and a practical application that you can implement immediately. Action is everything. It's one thing to read a motivational book, but it's another thing entirely to actually apply the principles to your life.

Whether it's in running, another sport, or the game of life, I hope to bring you encouragement, thought process, and tangible strategies for you to gain an edge in the specific goals and dreams that you aspire to accomplish.

My mission is to help you overcome your mental barriers so you can run your best race, live your best life, and achieve your dreams. I can guide you through the refining process so you can live to your fullest potential and become exactly who you were created to be. You are worthy, and it's your time.

My Calling

Step into your calling;
It's been there all along.
I've only been waiting
For you to hear the song.

You are the only one capable
To fulfill the role I've given,
So stop running away;
Step up and start living.

I long so much for you
To learn and change and grow
Into the person that
Only I truly know.

And now it's time for
The world to finally see
That when you step into your calling,
You'll be a reflection of Me.

Chapter 1

Nothing But Ordinary

"As the heavens are higher than the earth, so are my ways higher than your ways, and my thoughts than your thoughts."
– Isaiah 55:9

Bart Millard understands fighting for a dream. He also understands pain. His childhood was full of emotional and physical abuse. He was told he wasn't good enough and that following his dream was a stupid idea. His own father told him he'd never measure up! However, one of his high school teachers saw a fight in him that Bart didn't even know he had, and she took a chance on him. With her support, and a little push, he landed the lead role in a school play and began to explore his musical talent.

When record labels told his band they'd never make it, he wanted to quit, and he almost caved. However, something deep inside kept him fighting for his dream. His story is one of true redemption, and after making amends with his dad, he wrote a beautiful song portraying that redemption story called, "I Can Only Imagine." Bart Millard, of popular band Mercy Me, followed his dream with grit and pure determination despite his circumstances, and that song, which quickly turned number one, was just the launching pad for his successful musical career. The sheer amount of mental toughness he exerted to keep his dream alive was seemingly insurmountable.

The mind is a powerful tool. If we use it right, we may draw closer to what we are capable of, and the limitations we place on ourselves begin to vanish. Performing was a passionate pursuit for Bart Millard, and it made him feel alive.[1] What makes you feel that way? Do you have a dream that's been placed on your heart already? What is screaming at you from the inside wanting to come out and thrive?

You don't have to be a runner to enjoy and apply the principles laid out in this book. I am a runner, so naturally much of my experience and expertise is derived from that world. *Mind Over Marathon* is about discovering a dream and taking it from inception to a flourishing finish. This book is geared toward YOU, someone who has big dreams hidden deep within and wants to draw them out. My goal is to provide you with practical ways to accomplish that. I'll take you through the process of developing your dreams and the steps that it takes to actually execute a game plan so you can believe it and achieve it.

In order to get you where you want to go, I first need to take you back to where I was. I never aspired to be a runner. In fact, the thought of running any distance gave me the heebie-jeebies! My sport was basketball. Don't get me wrong—I wasn't a star basketball player by any means! Standing at barely five feet, I was deemed "too short", but I was a solid ball handler and three-point shooter, so I was valuable to the team as a point guard. I was quick and tough on defense, and I didn't mind getting in a player's face. When I caused an offensive foul on an opponent, I rejoiced on the inside because it meant I was that much quicker than the competition. The dribbling of the basketball and continuous stop and go of a game broke up the mundaneness of running. Shooting the ball and seeing it swoosh through the net was a sweet distraction because, to me, running was just not fun. In my eyes, running was simply meant for conditioning. When we messed up and had to run "killers" across the gym floor, over and over again, I associated running as a form of punishment rather than as a form of pleasure or sport. It wasn't in my nature—or so I thought at that point in my life.

I didn't go on to play college basketball, so ironically, I took up running as a way to stay active. Before I realized it, I had fallen in love with the peaceful solitude that running provided. I began to look forward to the feeling of the sun beaming down on me while on a pleasure run, surrounded by the vibrant colors of nature. It was a time of tranquility and reflection before the busy-ness of the day began. I no longer avoided it! Instead, I welcomed this newfound sport, as it became a new challenge for me. It's hard to describe why running brings me such joy, but when my feet hit the pavement, it's as though all the stresses in my day fade away, and I'm ready to embark on the challenges ahead. It's medicine to my soul.

In college, I had high ambitions and dreamed of becoming a famous sports broadcaster and author. I had a clear vision of what I wanted my life to look like. Of course, we all know that our plans don't always turn out exactly how we design. My plan was to be an independent and successful working woman in New York City. Instead, I got married immediately following college graduation and, a short year later, found out we were expecting our first baby.

I wouldn't change that path for anything, but I did end up putting my dreams on the back burner, and there they stayed for many, many years. Every year that went by seemed to bring me a year further from my dream, which, in turn, made the vision seem more and more distant and unattainable. Little did I know that there was a mental battle raging inside of me and maybe, just maybe, I was still destined for greatness on this new path I was traveling. It may not have been the path I had originally envisioned, but it could still be just as sweet. It was a precious reminder that the path we follow is the path God sets out for us, and we follow it in His time, not ours.

Now, fourteen years later, my husband and I have three very active and amazing young boys. In those early years, I told myself that my mission was to raise them. *But looking back now, could that have been an excuse? A reason for me not to pursue what I believe I was created to do?* Deep within, I began to realize that I never want my boys to have to look beyond me to find a role model—someone with passion to pursue goals and dreams, someone who won't give up when obstacles peek their nasty heads in all directions.

I have found that our lives can become so consumed with our kids, their needs, and their activities, that we forget that they are studying us and watching what we do in order to attain a picture of what life and success truly entail. If we're not willing to pursue our call, then how should we expect our kids to? I decided I needed to lead by example and GO GET MY DREAM! It was a matter of deciding once and for all that I would listen to and accept my call. I decided I would not back down. Wondering if it was too late to fulfill my aspirations was no longer valid.

Our dreams can change and evolve over time, but it's never too late to pursue them. It's never too late to live them out.

I had stopped running when I found out I was pregnant with our first son because the doctors told me I had a high-risk pregnancy, and they were worried I wouldn't have a full-term baby or even have him at all. I had an ovarian cyst that ruptured when I was a senior in high school, and through that painful process, we found out that my body was not set up correctly to bear the weight of a full-term pregnancy. Doctors told me I'd be lucky to conceive, but if I did, the chances were slim that the baby would survive. They assumed I would miscarry early on.

I held onto the promise of life, but I played it on the safe side and heeded instruction to take it easy. As the pregnancy progressed, I was monitored carefully because of minor preterm contractions caused by multiple infections I fought off throughout my pregnancy. A kidney infection landed me in the hospital for even closer observation. However, despite the doctor's worries, our oldest son was a healthy, full-term baby, and there were minimal complications throughout the pregnancy.

My newfound parenting journey came with two years of inactivity in comparison to the high-intensity exercise I was used to. Anything can become a habit, just like working out was a habit for me. When I took this hiatus from running, it became a habit to be sedentary. I had every intention to start back up, but it wasn't as easy as I had thought it would be.

When we found out I was pregnant with our second baby, because I had that knowledge and experience from the first pregnancy, I did remain active, but it wasn't until after he was born that I really had the drive to get back into pre-baby shape. I made up my mind to train for a half marathon because I enjoy the challenge of big goals—a shorter race didn't seem enough of a challenge. My training went fairly well, and I started to enjoy running as "me time" again. If you hadn't noticed, I'm the type of person who makes lofty goals and aspires to achieve big in all I do, so naturally, after that race, I resolved that a marathon was the next step. I was already halfway there, so why not?

Three months later, the 2010 Twin Cities Marathon sold me on running as a lifestyle. This race is often called "the most beautiful urban marathon in America" because it takes place in the beginning of October when the trees in Minnesota have turned brilliant colors, and the chill in the air usually makes for perfect running weather. The course begins in downtown Minneapolis and winds around popular city lakes, including Lake of the Isles, Bde Maka Ska (formerly Calhoun), Harriet, and Nokomis, and eventually heads up along the Mississippi River to historic Summit Avenue in St. Paul, where the finish line and State Capitol eventually meet.

Once I crossed the finish line at the State Capitol, I knew I was addicted to this newfound sport! The energy from the crowds was contagious. Cheering filled the air at every turn, and music blared throughout the course. I couldn't help but smile or giggle at the different signs that people were displaying: 'Run fast, I just farted!' 'Chuck Norris never ran a marathon.' 'This is a lot of work for a free banana.' So much support and encouragement flooded the streets, making me feel like a superstar accomplishing greatness. I felt invincible.

My next ambition—qualify for the Boston Marathon. The Boston Marathon is the oldest marathon in the country and recognized as America's iconic race. Runners can't just sign up to run, they have to qualify, which means they have to be fast. This marathon is considered to be one of the most difficult because of the hills in the latter part of the course, culminating with Heartbreak Hill, just shy of a half mile long, near Boston College.

In the running world, qualifying for Boston means running with some of the best in the sport. It's a way to distinguish yourself as "elite" among "normal runners." I love that! It seemed lofty but yet extremely exciting. Many aspire to run the Boston Marathon, but few make the decision to train with a "whatever it takes" mentality in order to qualify. That's the beauty of this sought-after marathon. The more engrossed I became in the running world, the more intense my dream of running the legendary Boston Marathon became. I had to do it. I had to get there.

I ran the Twin Cities Marathon again the next year, and I trained hard on my own but failed to hit my goal. I actually finished in about the same time as I had the year before. I was disappointed, but I knew I needed to train differently. So, I resolved to try again. That next summer, I planned to run Grandma's Marathon along Minnesota's North Shore from Two

11

Harbors to Duluth. This time, I found a coach, and I worked harder than ever before.

Having a coach was a major game changer, as he could be the voice into my running soul. He personalized my training and helped me to see things about my running that I needed to fix. He pushed me harder than I would have ever pushed myself on my own. I wanted to perform to validate his coaching, but I also wanted to perform to hold myself accountable to see what I was capable of. I wanted to see if I could reach my own potential.

I had a personal best time at Grandma's, three hours and fifty-one minutes, but it wasn't enough. I needed to run a Boston-qualifying (BQ) race in three hours and thirty-five minutes to qualify, which felt extremely distant. I cut my time by nineteen minutes from my previous marathon, but I still had to shave sixteen additional minutes to qualify for Boston. This may not sound like much, but dropping nineteen minutes is an exceptional accomplishment, as it is cutting about forty-five seconds off every mile. The problem was that I couldn't just count on hitting my qualifying time, rather I would need to beat it by as much time as possible to be guaranteed a racing spot in Boston.

Qualifications for the Boston Marathon are based on gender and age. In all actuality, I had to try cutting about twenty-one minutes off my time in order to achieve a Boston qualifying time that ensured my acceptance into the race. There is limited space, and they take the fastest runners in each age bracket until the race is filled to capacity. Twenty-one more minutes would mean dropping nearly one minute off my best mile pace.

At that point, feeling a bit defeated, I decided to hang up my dream for a while. As a battle raged inside my head, I started wondering if it were even possible. I mentally started shutting down, and negative thoughts of failure crept in. I slowed down and did a triathlon one year and a duathlon the year after that, but I wasn't satisfied. I knew I still had more inside. I was still hungry. I knew I was capable of more than I was putting out.

The 2013 Boston Marathon came, and I watched from afar, disappointed that I hadn't hit my goal to be at the starting line. That year was unlike any others, however, as it was the year of the horrific Boston Marathon Bombing. I had many friends message me wondering if I was there and asking if I was okay. The bombing killed three, including a little boy, and injured several others—many who ironically lost limbs.

This terrorist attack hit me hard; I knew I could have been right there among the victims. It resonated deep within my soul. It wasn't just an attack on the running community, it was an attack on the country that I love. A sense of pride for my country and for my fellow runners rose up inside me. The Boston Bombing drove a deeper internal desire to earn the opportunity to take my place at the start line. It may sound strange, but I sensed it was a sort of duty to get there, signifying we aren't scared and we won't back down.

We had our third baby in March of 2014, and I was getting the marathon itch again. I wanted so badly to do something for me, and I decided it was now or never. It was still a pipe dream of "maybe if it works," or "possibly it'll be my year," but I made the decision to give it a go one more time. Once I officially registered for my next marathon, I knew my decision was final. I was ready to pull out the "whatever it takes" mentality to turn this dream into reality.

A decision isn't a decision until it is backed by action. No longer would I say "maybe" or "possibly." In my spirit, it was no longer a wish. Rather, I knew it was my time, and this was necessary. I HAD to make it happen. Being decided means you take on a "whatever it takes" mentality, and you start filtering all of your choices through the lens of whether or not it will get you closer to your dream or goal.

The 2015 Grandma's Marathon was my chance to prove to myself that I'm a winner and that my dream is worth it. So what made the difference? How did I go from "giving it a shot" to "it's my time," and "I'm going to do it?" Do you need to take that step in achieving your dream?

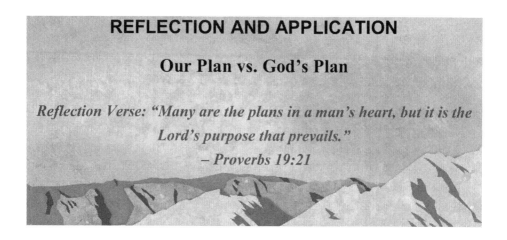

REFLECTION AND APPLICATION

Our Plan vs. God's Plan

Reflection Verse: "Many are the plans in a man's heart, but it is the Lord's purpose that prevails."
– Proverbs 19:21

God has a plan for our lives, and sometimes it is nothing like what we expected or pictured. He likes to use ordinary, weak, flawed people to do extraordinary things. If you are willing, He will lead you. He proves himself time and time again. God uses the ordinary to show His extraordinary. God uses the flawed to show His beauty. God uses the weak to show His strength. God uses the poor to show His wealth. His promises overrule the facts. With God, the facts just don't count:

- Abraham was too old

- Noah was a drunk

- Joseph was abused

- Moses stuttered

- Gideon was afraid

- Samson was a womanizer

- Rahab was a prostitute

- Jeremiah was too young

- Jacob was a cheater

- Leah was ugly

- David was a murderer

- Jonah ran from God

- Naomi was a widow

- Peter denied Christ

- Martha worried about everything

- Zacchaeus was small and greedy

- Paul persecuted Christians

- John the Baptist ate bugs

Reflection Questions:

1. What "character flaws" are you holding onto as a crutch?
2. What talents and gifts do you have that you can develop?
3. What do you feel God is calling you to do?
4. Are you ready to answer the call placed on your heart?
5. Are you ready to take your ordinary and let God do something extraordinary?

Further Reading:

- Isaiah 55:8-9

- Proverbs 3:5-6

- 2 Corinthians 12:9

- Philippians 4:13

Application:

1. Make a list of flaws you think you may have that keep you from moving forward.

2. Take a bold, black marker, and write Philippians 4:13 and 2 Corinthians 12:9 directly over the list of flaws. This is a reminder that we can do all things through Christ and that His grace is made perfect in our weakness.

3. Lastly, I want you to tear up that list and throw it away—or recycle it. What you see as weaknesses may no longer be used as an excuse. Weakness no longer defines you. God wants to use each of us in our weakness because that's when He gets the glory.

Chapter 2

Race Day

"Let us run with perseverance the race marked out for us."
– Hebrews 12:1

I could hardly sleep the night before the 2015 Grandma's Marathon. My stomach was in knots thinking about what was to come. I was extremely anxious but excited. I was nervous but hopeful. I was somewhat fearful but full of faith. All these mixed emotions were vying to take the lead role in the forefront of my mind. Let's be honest, I was a basket case on the inside with a smile on the outside. I had built up a dream, become passionate about achieving it, and now I knew it was time.

It's important to find something to be passionate about. It's important to have goals and dreams and aspire for success in THAT avenue. Why? Because you are worthy, you are strong, and you are capable of achieving more than you can imagine.

The weather wasn't promising, as dark clouds overhead threatened possible thunderstorms. I didn't let that change my outlook. I had a goal, I had a plan, and it was time to execute—rain or shine. I was as prepared as I was going to get. I was ready. I had spent months training. I had spent hours visualizing race day. I had sweat. I had cried. I had laughed. I trained through injury. I trained through pain. I trained when I was excited to. I trained when I really didn't feel like it. All the race preparation and training catered to my determination to win and not let anything get in the way. I honestly knew I was as prepared as I needed to be, so all these feelings and emotions—though very real—didn't need to dictate the outcome. It was time for my training to pay off.

Creating a game plan, following through with it, and trusting it is vital for any dream to become a reality. It starts with a larger dream, which is then broken down into smaller, achievable goals. These are stepping stones to attaining your long-term vision.

Grandma's Marathon is truly breathtaking as it offers some of Minnesota's most beautiful scenery along the North Shore of Lake Superior. It follows the scenic route from Two Harbors to Duluth, where runners cross the finish line in the famous Canal Park with a rewarding view of ships entering the harbor under the iconic Aerial Lift Bridge. Runners actually get their first glimpse of the Lift Bridge around mile eleven, which is deceiving, as there are still many miles remaining. I knew I'd get this view near the beginning and that it's a mind trick; however, it made me feel like I was closer than I was. It was quite a let down knowing I still had a good fifteen miles more to go. The waves of Lake Superior lapping the shoreline created for me a sense of peacefulness overriding my overly anxious thoughts! The shoreline seemingly chases runners throughout the race until they wind away into the streets of Duluth for the final few miles. The scenery was majestic, and I experienced a feeling of serenity as I made my way down the shore.

The morning of the race finally came, and I woke to cloud cover, but soon, it started to lightly rain. A little fear tried to creep in, telling me that the imperfect conditions would lead to failure. I shook it off and said it would be amazing despite the weather—deep down hoping that was the truth. I couldn't control the weather conditions. However, I could control my actions and my attitude.

You need to choose to focus on the things in your control and not worry about anything out of your control. Faith trumps fear. You need to have trust in your game plan.

We stayed at a rustic inn right off the start line in Two Harbors, Minnesota, so I used the bathroom one more time and headed to the start line just in time for the gun. As the National Anthem played in the background, butterflies filled my stomach. I realized this was my chance to prove that I am worthy and meant for more. It was also my chance to prove that it's never too late to reach higher, achieve more, or believe in greatness.

Often times, a challenge will stop you in your tracks and force you to back off. This leads to a mindset that it isn't meant to be, or you just don't have what it takes. But rising up and facing our giants head-on is the key to victory. Giants are put in your path to teach you something, to give you the chance for victory, to give you the opportunity to become better. It's your choice to fall under pressure or to get up, dust yourself off, and rise above your circumstances. Your breakthrough is on the other side of your giant.

You can't let the circumstances define you. Your testimony is on the other side of the wall in your way. You need to push through with a "whatever it takes" mentality to get to the other side. You need to dig deep and discover the strength you have down inside of you.

Before we even started, my feet were soaked from the heavy rain. But eventually, it settled into a light drizzle, which turned out to be perfect conditions to keep the temperature cool and the humidity down. I wasn't about to let a little water change my mind. I had to be mentally strong to not let the weather affect my attitude. Soaked feet equals sore feet, so I had to take my mind off the facts, or what many other people would consider the current circumstances. The facts just don't count. My circumstances didn't need to define me. After all, it's just skin.

When you are decided about your dream and are going after it with all you have, the facts don't count. Whatever it is that says you can't do it doesn't count because, if you press on toward your goal, the facts will change. Being decided—making and committing to the decision to finish— is an important first step to achieving any goal.

I felt good in the beginning. I was convinced I would achieve the goal I set out to do. I started out fast—maybe a little too fast—but that's how I seem to do things. I am a positive split kind of girl, and I have come to terms with that. Most runners work toward a negative split, which means they run the first half at a comfortable pace and then, if they are feeling good, try to speed up for the second half. I am quite the opposite. No matter how hard I try, I go out too fast in the beginning and hold strong the first half, but I slow down toward the end, creating a positive split. Mile three came, and my IT band injury started to flare up. I had issues with it during my training, but I had hoped to avoid issues during the race. I told myself I'd keep going either way. I had come way too far to quit. In the words of

New England Patriots Quarterback Tom Brady, "I didn't come this far to only come this far."

An IT band injury, also known as Iliotibial Band Syndrome, is one of the most common overuse injuries among runners. It transpires when the iliotibial band, the ligament that runs down the outside of the thigh from the hip to the shin, becomes tight or inflamed. The IT band attaches to the knee and helps with stabilization and movement of the joint. When the IT band isn't working properly, movement of the knee can become painful, which means running can become painful.[1]

IT band pain can be severe enough to completely sideline a runner for weeks. That is exactly the kind of pain I was experiencing, though it was through the hip and thigh where I was feeling the most pain. It was excruciating and probably would have sidelined the common runner. I was determined not to be a common runner. I was determined to beat it. Now, here's my disclaimer about running through injury. Some injuries or annoyances you can push through without doing too much damage or causing other problems. Others? Not so much. Pain serves a purpose, and sometimes we need to listen to our bodies and let them heal. I knew this pain wasn't going to cause lasting damage, and I chose to run through it.

You need to learn to get tough in all areas. To get through the circumstances, you need discipline in key areas: physical, mental, and emotional. You need to train your body to do what you tell it to do. Your body is your slave; you are not a slave to it.

By the 10k mark, I was at a 7:05 minute-per-mile pace and still feeling fine, but at the halfway point, not only was my IT band in pain, but my right calf had also tensed up from the rain and chill. I did beat my personal best half marathon time by almost six minutes though, so I had no doubt that if I could just fight through the pain, I'd hit my goal time. It was at that point that I had to dig deep and rely on the mental toughness I had built up throughout the previous months. I told myself if I could keep up the pace to mile twenty, then I could slow down a bit and still make it. I convinced myself of that. That very thought kept me going.

By mile twenty, the pain was so intense that even the simple act of lifting my legs was excruciating. I could barely get one foot in front of the other. It was an agonizing pain that could have been debilitating if I let it.

I kept telling myself it was only a little further and that I trained for this very moment. My breathing was just fine—great actually—and so was my endurance. I felt like I could keep going, but my legs told a different story. They were having a hard time pushing through. The injury to my IT band was enough to force me to slow down even though I didn't want to and even though my lungs screamed for me to keep the quick pace.

You need to cut off the negativity that creeps into your mind. When a negative thought comes, you need to learn to proactively speak positively toward it. You cannot accept any negative the mind brings. It can paralyze you from moving on if you let it.

Once we veered off scenic Highway 61, and away from Lake Superior, crowds formed in the streets to motivate and encourage us. Usually around mile twenty, many University of Minnesota-Duluth students are out cheering, and it is one of the loudest points of the race. The last six miles are usually the toughest, as many runners have hit their "wall" and are just praying for the finish line to come! The music, the signs, and the cheering were a sweet distraction. The vibrant energy of the crowd kept me going.

Community is so important. You need cheerleaders backing you up. You need a few key people speaking positive into your life. With community comes celebration.

The most pivotal point of the entire race—the turning point—was just after mile twenty-four when my friend Kristen was in the street screaming her head off for me through a megaphone, encouraging me to keep going. She knew I was in pain, she could see it written all over my face, and she helped me to find that extra burst to finish strong.

It is important to associate with others who either have what you want or are going in the same direction. You can feed off each other's drive and ambition. You can lift each other up and encourage one another. You can remind each other and reinforce the knowledge that your dreams are worth it, and you are strong and worthy enough to achieve them.

At that point, I honestly didn't know if my legs would keep turning over long enough to let me finish the race! But I decided that I needed to dig deep inside of me and pull out any and all positive thoughts and

21

feelings. I pulled out the visualization I used while training: Seeing myself crossing the finish line with a "3:30" on the clock. I thought back to the pain and toil of my many months of training. It took all I had to keep going and finish strong.

Visualization is key. Seeing it already done, especially when it doesn't seem like it will work, is vital. You need to pair visualization with an emotional component. Not only is it important to see yourself hitting your goal, but you also need to get yourself into the place to emotionally feel what it will be like when you hit your goal.

The last two miles seemed to take forever, as I had slowed way down, but the sight of the finish line was so sweet. When runners hit the final part of Harbor Drive and pass by the William A. Irvin, an ore boat turned into museum, their minds deceive them, and they think the finish is right there. In all actuality, there's still a good quarter mile to go.

The finish line was the most amazing scene that I had clearly pictured in my mind hundreds of times while training. The crowd of spectators lined the finishing chute with deafening cheers. I saw the clock with bright red numbers in front of me, ticking and tocking. My feet continued to turn over one step at a time. I even got one last burst of energy to sprint across the finish line within my goal time of three hours and thirty minutes. Seeing that exact time on the clock was emotional, something I envisioned daily in training. I had imagined seeing "3:30" on the clock as I finished each training workout. I had seen it so many times in my mind that it was destined to become reality.

Once my feet crossed under the finisher's archway, I broke down. Tears streamed rapidly down my cheeks, and I was at a loss for words. I had played what it would feel like over and over in my head, and it felt exactly as I had imagined—maybe even better. I had such an intense visualization of crossing the finish line that in my training when I pictured it, I teared up just as I had on the actual day. It was a surreal feeling knowing that the dedicated hours I had trained for finally led to my dream coming to fruition. It was an intense moment of accomplishment and pride, coupled with pain and exhaustion.

It's an amazing feeling when you crush your goals. It's a rush knowing all the hard work paid off and was worth it. When you crush your goals, you naturally inspire others to become better as well. You show them that dreams aren't just dreams—they can be turned into accomplishments with the right training—physically and mentally.

The beauty of a marathon is that the lessons within relate to all areas of life. You don't have to be a runner to apply these same principles to your own goals and dreams. They will work for anyone who chooses to work them. You just have to be willing.

Qualifying for the Boston Marathon was the most amazing feeling in the world. I had done it. I beat the demons that tried to creep in. I beat the pain I physically felt. I beat the weather trying to rain on my parade—literally. It was then that I truly realized that the physical training is only a sliver of the battle. A mental boot camp to flush the negative and keep the emotional ping pong in check is just as important, if not more. That is what I stand on—the power of our thoughts and words and the ability for them to either build us up or tear us down. It's our choice.

REFLECTION AND APPLICATION

It's Never Too Late

Reflection Verse: "Do you not know that in a race all the runners run, but only one gets the prize? Run in such a way as to get the prize."
— 1 Corinthians 9:24

The enemy loves to lie! He loves to scream at us that we are not worthy, we are too young or too old, we are not equipped, or we'll never make it. As difficult as it can be, we need to ignore those screams and listen for God's gentle whispers of truth. It is never too late to reach higher, to achieve more, to believe in greatness. God doesn't call the equipped; He equips the called. You are worthy, and you are meant for more. No matter what lies the enemy may be throwing your way, it's not too late for you to rise up.

Reflection Questions:

1. What do you think you are capable of?

2. What lies has the enemy told you that you have believed?

3. What truths is God whispering to you today?

4. How can you find the inner strength to rise up and take action?

5. Where do you find power and strength when it seems everything is telling you to stop?

Further Reading:

- Isaiah 40:28-31

Application:

1. Write down all the lies you are hearing the enemy pronounce about you.
2. Next to each lie, write a truth from God's Word that shuts that lie down.
3. Place this list in a spot you can come back to whenever those lies creep in so you can reflect on God's truth in your life.

Examples:

Lie: I am not worthy.

God's Truth: I am worthy because I am the princess of a King (Galatians 3:26).

Lie: I'm too young.

God's Truth: I'm never too young to be an example in speech, conduct, love, and faith (1 Timothy 4:12).

Lie: I don't have the finances.

God's Truth: My God shall supply all my needs according to His glorious riches (Philippians 4:19).

Chapter 3

Dare To Dream

"If you don't have a dream, how can you have a dream come true?"
— Jiminy Cricket

J.K. Rowling was a single mom living on welfare and trying to provide for her daughter after a divorce. She literally had nothing going for her, and nothing to give. But, she also didn't let that keep her from dreaming. It took her seven years to write *Harry Potter and the Sorcerer's Stone*, and twelve major publishers rejected her book! Did she give up on her dream at that point? We all know the answer to that. After completing the seven-book Harry Potter series and helping produce the latter films, she became the world's first billionaire author. Even when it looked like there was no hope, she refused to turn in—from rags to riches, she fought through and achieved her dreams![1]

Have you ever imagined doing something so big it scared you, and you had no idea how you'd accomplish it on your own? While that might feel like an impractical idea, this is often how the best dreams start. The real dreams, the life-changing dreams, start when you dream huge. You need a dream so big that you can't imagine how it will come together on your own. A dream large enough that it frightens you. A dream far bigger than yourself.

WHAT MAKES UP A DREAM

Ultimately, you want to find a dream that seems impossible, but it's okay to have smaller dreams along the way. Smaller dreams can aid you in your pursuit of the larger, long-term desire. Dreams help you become passionate about the work you must do to attain them. Dreams keep you feeling alive, they spark a fire in your life, and they give you something to look forward to.

Why Should We Dream?

When we dream, we're ultimately finding purpose in our lives. Dreamers have hope. Dreamers create. Dreamers inspire. When we seek out our purpose and walk into our calling, things often feel less tough. When we dream and walk in our purpose, we find joy in the otherwise minutiae of work.

We were created to work. We were created to achieve. When we are walking in that, when we are dreamers, we can genuinely enjoy getting up in the morning. We can enjoy our work because we know it is purposeful and holds meaning. It drives us forward.

When we don't have a dream, our work feels tough and unenjoyable. It can lead us into a downward spiral of unfulfillment and depression. We can take our frustrations out on those we love the most. Personally, I'm much more irritable with those closest to me when I'm off the path of my dream. When I'm not striving toward a goal, I automatically become more angry and edgy. Working without a purpose can pull us into a negative mindset and create a "woe is me attitude."

Ever since I was little, I dreamt of writing a book. I knew I could be inspirational in my writing, but I let negativity and lies keep me from pursuing that vision I had for my life. It wasn't until recently, when I made the decision that it was my time, and I needed to step into my calling— pursue my dream—that I began to fully feel alive again. When my passion became my work, what I was doing no longer felt like work. We need to dream so we can stay passionate. We need to dream so we are always full of hope and can use our potential to do good. Dreamers solve problems. Dreamers create beauty in this world.

Defining A Dream

What is a dream, anyway? A dream is a "cherished aspiration, ambition, or ideal."[2] When was the last time you just sat and contemplated what you want your life to be like or who you want to become? Have you ever imagined an accomplishment coming to fruition? Do you get lost in a trail of daydreams? If not, why? Have you given up on the idea that you could do more, become more?

I've experienced many times when fear crept in and made my dreams seem foolish or made me feel as though I wasn't good enough to accomplish them. Sometimes I have grandiose dreams and too many of them, so I never actually latch onto one and see it through.

Let's break this definition of "Dream" down even further. To *cherish* is "to hold dear" to something, and *aspiration* is "a hope or ambition of achieving something." An *ambition* is "a strong desire to do or to achieve something typically requiring determination and hard work," and an *ideal* is "a person or thing regarded as perfect." Therefore, a dream comes from holding dear to a hope and strong desire of achieving something regarded as perfect, which requires determination and hard work.[3]

That is a loaded definition, but what I find profound is that a dream is a hope or a strong desire. It takes more than just having a dream to succeed, but it still is the indispensable first step in the process. What is screaming at you from the inside wanting to come out and thrive?

Dreams And Goals Are Not The Same

I want to make a distinction between a dream and goal because, though they appear similar in nature, they are quite different. Dreams are something we think about doing, when we let our imagination run wild with possibilities. Sometimes they're realistic and sometimes they're what most would call "crazy." They are the aspirations of our heart that if we knew we had the means to do them, we'd jump on the chance. Yet, they continue to be just a daydream without the action behind them.

Goals are what we are acting toward. They are our dreams working themselves out, driven by the force of our actions. Goals are broken down into a well-thought out plan that can bring our dreams into reality. They are the building blocks, or stepping stones, toward our wildest dreams. They are the necessity behind our dreams coming true.

Small vs. Large Dreams

Small dreams are an essential piece to the larger vision, but they are not a substitute for a big dream. They help keep us on track and break the process down into milestones along the way. Smaller dreams motivate the short-term vision and enable us to continue moving forward and making progress. However, I believe that there are three major dangers that come when we only have a small dream:

1. It isn't motivating to complete a small dream. Where there isn't a burning reason why, there is complacency. A small dream won't always get you out the door, eager to do the work it will take to finish.

2. A small dream does not challenge you. The lack of a challenging goal makes us think that we don't need to start now. It can be a means for procrastination. A weak WHY allows us to take our time and get it done whenever. There is no sense of urgency.

3. A small dream can be completed entirely on our own, which means we rely on our own ability and discipline. When it's not easily completed by yourself, there is more drive to get in the fight *and* bring others along with you.

Small dreams are not a bad thing, but a larger, more developed dream gives us more to strive for. It gives us a long-term vision and takes us out of our comfort zone, demanding we grow and change. A large dream takes more courage and gumption. Accomplishing a large dream will give us more satisfaction than a simple, easily achievable dream. There are three main reasons a challenging dream may be more beneficial than a smaller, easily achieved goal:

1. Larger dreams have less competition. More people choose to be average rather than pursue something greater than themselves. If you choose to be average, you remain in a sea of ordinary where everyone blends in and goes with the flow. It's harder to make something interesting that has been done a zillion times. Why not choose to think bigger and take the path less traveled?

2. People are more likely to help you achieve larger dreams than to aid in minuscule ones. Others want to feel like they belong and are a part of something bigger. It's more probable that family and friends will stand by you as you work toward a higher goal because it's more likely you will need or ask for advice and help. Everyone wants to feel needed, and a larger dream will require more out of others.

3. You'll find out what you're made of. Your character will be revealed as you withstand obstacles and distractions along the way. Anything worth reaching for will not come without a fight. There will be bumps in the road and issues you didn't foresee, but if you stick with it, and see it through, you'll find that you are capable of more than you imagined. Stepping out of your comfort zone leads to a stronger, more tenacious you. It takes faith to risk more.

When hunting rabbits in tiger territory, hunters need to be on a constant lookout for tigers. However, when hunting tigers in a rabbit territory, hunters can ignore all the rabbits. They're harmless! A big dream can make small "problems" seem to just go away because you're focused on the tigers (big dream) rather than the rabbits (problems).

DISCOVER AND DEVELOP YOUR DREAM

Sometimes the biggest hurdle is figuring out how to dream or what to dream. Committing to a dream is a big deal, and it can be overwhelming to know where to start, or underwhelming if you can't think of anything at all. What's nagging you on the inside? What is it that gets you fired up? What stirs you? What gets you emotional? Those are a few keys to figuring out what your dream could be. I wanted to be a fearless role model for my growing boys, and I wanted to take my running to the next level. The idea of running the Boston Marathon brought those two desires together, and that passion grew inside me until I couldn't ignore it.

How Do You Get A Dream?

What goals do you have? Or are you struggling to find a goal right now? There are many categories to choose from: health and fitness, career, travel, retirement, financial, spiritual, self-development, goals for your kids, and so many more. You can have dreams and goals in multiple categories. Don't sell yourself short. These categories can interweave within each other.

For example, say my large goal is to lose thirty pounds. My main category would be health and fitness. I would need to come up with a workout plan and a nutrition plan. I'd have to decide if I needed to hire a trainer. But it would stream into other categories as well because I would be working on self-development to change my mentality about health and fitness. When I hit my weight loss goal, I may reward myself with a fun trip I've always wanted to go on.

It's great to have dreams in all those categories! We will focus our attention on one or two at a time, but always keeping your dream tank full is how you stay motivated and continue to move forward. Find other people pursuing a BIG dream and associate with them, even if their dream is different from yours. You can feed off each other, grow together, encourage each other, and pursue greatness together.

Childlike Faith

Anne Shirley from the Anne of Green Gables series had such a vivid imagination, which seemed to always lead her into trouble. I believe that's what appealed to a majority of readers. It allowed them, at least for a moment, to step out of their daily strife and be able to see possibilities and cling to her adolescent longings.

Marilla, her caretaker, on the other hand, was quite the opposite. She wouldn't allow herself to see outside of her immediate reality. It's as though the music inside her had died a long time ago, and she shut off the ability to find joy in daydreams or even in life.

Why is it that as children, we could easily dream up what our future would look like, but as adults, we settle for mediocre, average lives? It's as though we move from childhood to adulthood and get so bogged down with life and responsibilities that we simply forget how to dream. Is there a reason WHY children lose the ability to dream? Do society and parenting play a role in children losing their ability to dream?

When I was a child, I didn't tell my parents I wanted to grow up and sit in a cubicle for nine hours a day, go home at night to watch television, go to bed, and do the same thing over again the next day and the next. No, I dreamt of success. I dreamt of doing something significant. I dreamt of leaving a legacy. I dreamt of being the one on the television, not merely watching it.

My oldest son doesn't tell me he wants to go to college to get into debt, find an average job, be an average person, and do average things. No, he dreams of success as well. He sees himself competing in the 2028 Olympics for USA Men's Gymnastics. He says he would go to college on a full-ride scholarship to pursue his gymnastics, but if the Olympic Training Center gave him an invite, he would choose to go there in a heartbeat.

Maybe that's why God tells us to have childlike faith. A child's innocent thinking, along with trust and belief, is massively powerful. It's as though when we move into adulthood, we're expected to put blinders on those dreams and join the daily grind. We are taught to go to school, get a good job, and join the rat race for the next forty to fifty years. Our monotonous daily routine overpowers us, casting a shadow on our childish faith and hope for our future.

Soon those blinders aren't even necessary because a slow fade comes over our dreams, and, before we know it, we've lost the ability to imagine huge—or even at all. When we are trying to reconnect with our passion and ability to dream, it helps to re-engage with that childlike faith. What did you dream about as a child? What did you look forward to? Try to let go of your grown-up expectations and blinders and let your imagination run wild.

Future Focused

Being a dreamer means you become future focused. Dreamers look ahead to what's to come. Dreamers fix their eyes on what could be—even what should be. In Philippians 3:14, Paul laid out the very being of dreamers when he said, "But one thing I do: Forgetting what is behind and straining toward what is ahead, pressing on toward the goal to win the prize for which God has called me heavenward in Christ Jesus."

We can learn from our past, but if we dwell in it, we will stay in it. While writing this book, I often looked back and thought, "Why didn't I get serious about my passion years ago? What if I did?" We can get caught up in the "may have been," but it's not a place to stay. I can't change anything I did or didn't do. I can only change what I will do. If I had written this book a few years back, I wouldn't have had the experience or examples that I do now. I also wasn't as emotionally stable and confident as I am now. Hindsight shows me that within the perceived struggles of the previous years, I've been preparing for such a time as this without even really realizing it.

Do you continue to look back and say, "If only I did *this*, then *that* could have been?" If only I would have gone to college, then I'd have a better job. If only I would have trained harder, then I could have played NCAA. If only! If only! We can't do that to ourselves because the minute we do, we think negatively about where we are and begin to think we can never get to where we want to go. Every moment, good or bad, can be a defining moment for our lives. Everything you have been through has helped you to become the person that you are today. Do you find yourself saying, "My life could have looked much different if I only would have…?"

When I catch myself doing this, I quickly look at what I wouldn't have if my life indeed did look differently. If I hadn't married my husband, I wouldn't have these three boys. The thin thread of how and why things happen and come together is too hard to explain or question. I don't want to look at life through the "what ifs." I want to look at it through the lens of "what can be." Let's move away from the past and into the future of possibilities.

BE DECIDED

Cinderella sang it perfectly, "A dream is a wish your heart makes." A dream is exactly that, just a wish, just a forethought. That is, until we decide to act on it. To turn a dream into reality, there absolutely needs to be a firm, unwavering decision.

It Starts With A Definite Decision

Until you intentionally decide that you are going after your dream, it's just a wish. This is where most of us miss it. Dreaming about running the Boston Marathon could have seemed silly to most, but it was a stirring desire inside me, and it turned into a passionate pursuit. It was a proving ground to me that I could still dream and have childlike faith. To make my dream a reality, I needed to set my intention, make the decision that I would do whatever it takes, and commit to seeing it through. I needed to turn my dream into a goal and go after it. As author Harvey Mackay said, "A dream is just a dream. A goal is a dream with a deadline and a plan."

For my first marathon, my goal was to finish. Running a marathon was on my dreams list, so I fought and trained and finished. But there's something about that runner's high, even though I felt incredibly depleted of all energy and downright terrible crossing the finish line, my heart stirred to increase my dream and pursue another goal—a lofty one.

Accomplishing an initial dream can open your eyes to what is possible and spur you on to the next dream, a dream larger than the previous. So if you don't have a dream yet, or if you've lost the ability to dream, don't worry about it. Start small. A small dream may seem colossal to you at this moment if, along the way, you've lost the dreamer inside. Once you accomplish that smaller dream, you'll restart the process and naturally begin to dream bigger and pursue larger ones until your dreams become bigger than yourself and look rather impossible on paper. It's a process, and we all have to start somewhere. I started with a 5k, then a half marathon, then a full marathon, then a spark led me to the crazy idea to qualify for the Boston Marathon. Each time a dream comes true, our vision expands, and we see so many more possibilities.

I dabbled in the thought of qualifying for the Boston Marathon because that seemed like the next step. This marathon is deemed extra special in the running world, as those aspiring to run in the race need to qualify based on strict times depending on age and gender. It is considered the cream of the crop in races, and if you run it, you become a part of an exclusive group of runners.

At first, I merely dabbled with the idea, which means it was a, "Well, if it happened, that'd be pretty neat," mentality. At that stage, I had dreamed up a cool thought, but I hadn't truly made a decision. Because of that, my training, my commitment, and my discipline were all lacking. My focus wasn't there, and I didn't make it the first time I "tried" for it. I really didn't even shave any time off from my first marathon. I finished about two minutes faster than my previous time, which was off my necessary qualifying time by thirty-five minutes. In the running world, thirty-five minutes is an enormous chunk of time to still have to shave off, as it requires cutting about a minute and a half per mile.

I didn't even make it the second time I "tried" for it. I may have taken more steps, including hiring a trainer, but I still had the mental ping-pong telling me the negative things that could happen. When it comes to making a decision, it's like Yoda said, "Do or do not; there is no try." *Be honest, you just read that quote in your head with Yoda's voice!* A decision means choosing to be decided no matter what. No swaying. No back door. No turning back.

The Facts Don't Count

When the dream is big enough, the facts—the perception of our current circumstances—don't count. The facts told me I needed to shave sixteen minutes off my time to just barely qualify. Putting this into perspective, my first marathon finish time was four hours and twelve minutes. My Boston qualifying time was three hours and thirty-five minutes, which was a difference of thirty-seven minutes just to qualify! That is almost a minute and a half I would have to shave off each mile.

Just running a qualifying time isn't always enough because they accept the fastest in each age group first and have limited space. I ran my third marathon in three hours and fifty-one minutes. To ensure I secured a running spot, I calculated that I'd have to run twenty-one minutes faster than my best time to date. Most would have looked at that and said no way and, frankly, probably would have quit.

The facts said I was too busy. I have three young boys, one was under a year old at the time. I was homeschooling and working multiple part-time jobs. The facts said I didn't have the time to commit to a rigid training schedule. But when the dream is big enough, the facts don't count. I chose to schedule my runs into my day and lose a little sleep. I chose not to use my boys as an excuse to not get my workouts in. I chose to look beyond the facts and focus on my dream.

When the dream is so big that you can't do it on your own, then the facts can't count. Don't let the naysayers steal your dream and tell you that you'll never make it. Your dream matters. You matter. God wants you to accomplish your dream in mighty ways.

Excuses

Even when we've fully committed to our dream, at some point we will be tempted to hide behind an excuse. Even the biggest achievers are tempted to use excuses. The best that we can do is be prepared for the excuses that might come our way.

What are some common excuses people have as to why they haven't started or finished in the pursuit of their dreams? What holds people back from accomplishing their goals? Why are dreams that seem bigger than ourselves scary to start? I've heard many excuses and even used some of them myself. *I'm too old. I'm too young. I'm starting too late. People have already done this. Nobody's done this. I don't have the education. I don't have the experience. I don't have the time. I don't have the resources. I don't have the support.* You name it, it's been said. But no matter the excuse, all of them boil down to three common fears.

1. Fear of failure: It's hard to fail at something you never start. Failure is one of the greatest fears people have, and it can stop them in their tracks. In our success-driven culture, failure has been made notorious. It is not looked favorably upon. In the office, we get

reprimanded when we mess up. We get a strike on our profile, and you can only get a few before you're booted out and replaced. This may seem like a logical system, but it ignores a crucial fact. Failure is a necessary means to success. The most successful people have been the best at failing. Take Babe Ruth for example. He had 714 career home runs, which is phenomenal. But you know what? He also led the American League in strikeouts five times with an accumulation of 1,330 throughout his major league career. That's almost twice as many strikeouts to home runs! He failed almost 50 percent of the time! Yet, he's one of the most memorable baseball players of all history, and he was elected to the Hall of Fame. Kids imitate him, and adults commemorate him.[4] Many people are afraid to try new things because they are afraid of failure. But failure doesn't have to be a bad thing, failure is good. It's a learning ground. Take that failure and grow from it.

2. Fear of what others think: No matter how often people say they don't care what others think, they really do. They want everyone to like them and no one to disagree with them. The problem with this mindset is that, if you follow your passions, most likely, there will be someone out there who just doesn't like you or what you stand for. All successful people have critics, but they've learned to develop a thick skin and persevere through. The more influential you are, the more limelight you will get, which also means the more critics. Nelson Mandela, Mother Teresa, and Martin Luther King, Jr. all had something in common. They cared more for the cause they were fighting for than about what anyone else thought about them, and each of them paved the way for change. But I bet if you "Googled" them, you'll find hundreds and thousands of critics who said terrible things about each of them. When people care too much about what others think, it's a sign of low self-esteem. Let's think about this fear logically. We sit around concerned about what others might be thinking about us, but the truth is they most likely aren't even thinking about us at all because

they are dealing with their own life situations. When you know who you are and become okay with that, you move from caring about image and to pursuing what you know you were meant to do.

3. Fear of the unknown: The path less traveled is usually the harder one. You never know what will be around the corner. It's unfamiliar territory, which makes us uncomfortable. The unknown takes us out of our comfort zone and into a place of change. Let's get real, no one likes change! We love predictability. We love routine. The unknown is a scary place. However, change can only happen in the unknown—when we leave our comfort zone and are willing to grow.

Excuses don't show up when we are excited about a dream. They sneak in when we are down and exhausted. Understanding the root fears behind every excuse will help you to recognize and stop those doubts when they creep in.

PROTECT YOUR DREAM

It's important to protect your dream from anything that may try to steal your passion. There are many things that try to take over. *Our circumstances*. When things go wrong, the natural reaction is to retreat. *Self-imposed limitations*. We are our worst enemies at times. We sometimes set limits to what we believe we are capable of. We drag ourselves down not believing we are worthy enough to succeed. *Past track record*. Maybe we have started and stopped so many times that we no longer feel we are able to finish. Maybe we feel like we've made too many mistakes that we'll never get it right. *We care too much about what others think*. That's right. We never get started because we're trying so hard to be perfect. We don't want to have others see our weaknesses or imperfections. We're too worried about fitting in and being normal. Ultimately, only you can protect your dream. You have to recognize when something or someone is sneaking in to steal it.

Dream Makers vs. Dream Takers

I implore you to surround yourself with those who will lift you up and support your dream. Those people are dream makers. They believe in you and may even help you believe in yourself. Weed out anyone else—also known as the dream takers. A dream maker is uplifting and encouraging; a dream taker tears you down. A dream maker sees the positive; a dream taker shares only negative. A dream maker believes in you; a dream taker belittles you. A dream maker wants you to be the best version of you; a dream taker wants you to play it safe.

A dream taker can be a parent who said you weren't good at math. A dream taker could be a teacher who said you were a distraction, or a friend who thinks your head is in the clouds. A dream taker can be subtle or apparent, but you can spot them when someone belittles you or your dream. A dream taker may honestly believe he or she has your best interest in mind. He doesn't want to see you fail, so he prefers you don't even start.

What if Oprah listened to her grandma whose hopes for her were to become a maid someday for a nice white family?[5] What if Michael Jordan quit after being cut from his high school varsity basketball team?[6] Did you know that the concert hall manager at Nashville's Grand Ole Opry told Elvis Presley that he should go back to truck driving? What if he had listened to him?[7] What if Albert Einstein decided he wasn't good enough after being rejected by the Zurich Polytechnic School? Side note, he didn't even speak until he was four years old or read until he was seven![8] What if Lucille Ball of "I Love Lucy" listened to her drama instructors and chose a different profession?[9] Each of these icons chose to rise above the dream takers in their lives.

A dream taker is often someone who has settled for average in life. Sometimes it's hard for them to see someone else who wants to achieve more. They'd rather bring you down to average with them, so they don't have to feel bad about being complacent.

It's important to be careful with whom you share your desires and dreams because people don't always respond the way we hope they will. They aren't always immediately thrilled for us, and sometimes they would rather rain on our parade and share more negative emotions. Sometimes you sharing your vision reminds them of their lack of one. They make their negative response a defense mechanism for their shortcomings. They may be feeling guilty about a dream or goal they've had that they haven't done anything about. Your pursuit of success calls out their average ways.

As you chase your dreams, you'll inspire others to start dreaming again. Let the naysayers watch from afar, but don't let them drag you down. If you keep doing what you're doing and set yourself on fire, people will come out of the woodwork to watch you burn. Fan the flame for them but don't let them have a negative influence over you.

Choose to surround yourself with a few like-minded friends who are also looking to achieve more. When taking advice, ensure that person has what you want. Make sure that person is a dream maker. Make sure that person is continually working to better herself. We'll draw this idea of accountability and community out further in later chapters, and we'll also dive into the reality that there may be negative people in your life, specifically a parent or spouse, that you can't just cut out.

Controlling Your Thoughts

Negative thoughts can distract you from your dream and take you off course. They can lead to a downward spiral and paralyze you from going after your dreams. What is the purpose of negative thoughts? Can we take those thoughts and use them to our advantage instead? Where do they come from? How can we identify them before they create the downward spiral? How can we put a "bouncer" at the door of our mind? How do we begin to talk to ourselves if we have already spiraled downward with negative thoughts? These are all questions we will answer in a later chapter, but they're important to get us thinking right now. If we don't get control of our thoughts, we will have a hard time moving forward and accomplishing any goal we set out for ourselves.

The Problem With Multiple Dreams At Once

You can't be all in with multiple dreams. A big dream requires total focus. When you make a decision to pursue your dream, distractions will come. Notice I did not say distractions might come. I said they WILL come, guaranteed. Things that look appealing will magically appear

41

disguised as opportunities. They will look good, feel good, taste good. They will seem worthy of your time and attention.

But beware! When distractions come, you have a serious choice to make. Will you let them take you off the course, or will you discipline yourself to stay focused? Sometimes we want to say yes to what might seem good without really giving it more thought. However, sometimes we need to say no to what seems good in order to see God's best.

Maybe a job promotion comes up, and you decide to take it because you think the added finances will aid in your dream. When in reality, the additional time investment and responsibilities of the job take your focus off your dream and lead you away from pursuing it. I'm not saying job promotions are bad, rather I am saying keep in mind that distractions will be disguised as opportunities, and it's up to us to discern what is maybe only good and be willing to wait on what is best.

FINAL STRETCH

A dream is much more difficult to give up on when sacrifice and investment have been put toward it. When in pursuit of a dream, the investments made can include time, money, emotional energy, and heart, just to name a few. Don't worry, though. The sacrifice and investment to see your dream to fruition will be completely worth it. Find a trusted friend or fellow dreamer, let them in on your dream, and have them remind you regularly what your "why" is to keep you motivated and in pursuit of it—and go after your dream!

Discover Your Dreams

Reflection Verse: "And we know that in all things God works for the good of those who love him, who have been called according to His purpose."
– Romans 8:28

They say, "Get your head out of the clouds!" Two thoughts on that:

1. Who is "they," and why do they have such control of you in your life? The only opinion that matters is God's.

2. The only people who have made a lasting impact or created change are those who let their imaginations run wild.

God is the originator of the dreams in our heart. He gives us the desires to fulfill our purpose. Dare to dream. Dare to let others see you as a bit crazy. Dare to not fit in. Joseph's brothers ridiculed him—even sold him off—because he was a dreamer. Yet, he eventually became second to Pharaoh and saved the land from a massive famine—all because he was a dreamer and allowed God to flow through him. Dream a dream large enough that you need God's help to accomplish it. A dream big enough that you can't take the credit for the finished product, a dream where God receives the glory.

Reflection Questions:

1. As a child, what did you want to do when you grew up? What were some aspirations you had?
2. When did you stop allowing yourself to dream? Do you remember? How old were you?
3. Do you know what triggered your unbelief? Did someone or something make you feel like your dream wasn't good enough?
4. What's nagging you on the inside? What keeps you up at night?
5. What is it that gets you fired up? What stirs you? What makes you emotional?

Further Reading:

- Genesis 37 & 41
- 1 Timothy 4:12
- 2 Corinthians 10:5
- Psalm 37:4

Application: Create your 100 dreams list

- Think of it like a bucket list, but I prefer to call it a dreams list because that is a more positive spin. Throw everything you have ever wanted to do, see, or have on the list. It will not be easy to fill all 100 spots, but do it! Think from the smallest of dreams to the impossible. This will help you begin to dream again and see hope for the future.

- Some questions to get you started: Where do you want to live? What kind of house do you want? Do you want multiple houses? Do you want land? Do you want to travel? Where do you want to travel? What do you want to see? What experiences do you want to have? What memories do you want to make? How much money do you want to make? Do you want to do anything for your parents? How about your siblings? What kind of toys do you want to have? Do you want a personal chef? Do you want a housekeeper? Do you want to give money away? To whom? How much? What can you imagine? The possibilities are endless.

Note: You can find the 100 Dreams Worksheet at

www.redhotmindset.com/MOMresources

Chapter 4

Fix Your Eyes

"The only thing worse than being blind is having sight but no vision."
– Helen Keller

One of my friends has a son who loves hockey and is the goalie for his team. In that position, he needs precision and vision to be effective deflecting the puck. She recently shared with me that he just got glasses that fit under his helmet, and it's made a world of difference. He refused contacts and said he thought he could see just fine. She took his word for it, but he didn't know what he didn't know.

He was used to his blurred vision and lived through it. It was his normal. But once he got these new glasses, a whole new world opened up to him. The puck seems to now magnetize to his glove. With clear vision, he's playing more to his potential, and he looks like a whole new goalie! When our vision is clear, the world is opened up to us. We have a fuller perspective and can see things from all angles. We can more easily see the path toward our dreams.

WHAT IS A VISION?

A vision is meant to be a long-term picture of a larger dream you want to see happen. A strong vision is larger than yourself, the capability to optimistically see yourself in a place you can't claim to be true right now. When you develop a clear vision, it helps you to pursue those passions and achieve the long term goals. A strong vision can connect your passions with your potential and endless possibilities. There is no purpose without vision.

Defining Vision

A vision is "the ability to think about or plan the future with imagination or wisdom."[1] It is a clear mental image, vivid in nature that depicts what the future could hold if you latch on. It becomes powerfully realistic as you ingrain the pictures of that vision in your mind.

Vision is a necessary tool for accomplishing all significant goals. Not only does it help you see what your life will be like having accomplished that goal, but also why it is imperative that the specific dream or goal come to fruition. What benefit beyond yourself comes from accomplishing your vision?

Did you notice that the definition included the word wisdom? Wisdom is "the quality of having experience, knowledge, and good judgment."[2] A vision isn't nonsensical or dreamsical. A vision is carefully planned out. It is backed with experience and knowledge. A visionary needs to have a sound mind with good judgment.

In the frigid Minnesota winters, some drivers, in a frenzy to get to their desired destination, scrape a minuscule hole in the layer of ice plastered on their windshields. In our hurried society, many have a microwave mentality and rush from here to there without clear direction. They're worried about being late to work or to an event or wherever they may be headed. They're afraid of missing out. However, the problem with this practice is that the tiny hole prevents drivers from having a full vision of the road. They can't clearly see all that is in front of them, thus, creating even more problems or delays throughout their drive.

Just as without a clear windshield drivers don't have a full view of the road ahead, a person working toward a goal without vision loses sight of the most direct path. A vision is the capability to see beyond your current reality into what could be. It creates a picture of what you want to have and who you want to become. It's you foreseeing your future and what it could hold.

Why A Vision?

Without a vision, you'll get stuck where you're at. That's what the Proverb means when it says, "Where there is no vision, the people perish."[3] If you don't see where you are going, then how are you going to get there? You need to have a clear view of what lies ahead and what you are trying to achieve. You need direction. You need to make sure your windshield is cleared of ice so you have a full view of the road.

A vision helps you to see past your current circumstances. It helps you envision life as it could be, not as it currently is. It can pull you toward your dreams and encourage your imagination to grow. The here and now tells a story, but it doesn't have to define where we end up. We can change the direction of our lives, and it starts with our imagination!

A vision calibrates your priorities. When you have determined where you want to go and can see it clearly, you will begin to arrange your priorities to line up with arriving at your destination. You'll begin to see through the lens of, "Will this get me closer to my dream or not?" You'll begin using this question to evaluate all of your choices and events you consider adding to your schedule.

A vision keeps you focused on what you want and keeps you motivated to achieve it. When you have clear direction, you will have a clear focus. With a vision, you're more likely to make the necessary changes to obtain your goal.

The Mind/Brain Connection

Dr. Caroline Leaf, a well-known cognitive neuroscientist, has done more than twenty years of research on the mind and brain connection, and what she has found is that the mind and brain are two very different and separate things that happen to work together. For a long time, scientists thought that the mind and brain were one and the same. The good news behind them being separated is that you can literally change your brain with every thought you are thinking. Your mind is how you think and feel and choose, not your brain.

Research has shown that the way that we think affects our physical and mental health by 75 to 98 percent. Dr. Leaf points out that the mind works through the brain, and the brain responds to the mind. You can control your reactions and make the brain work for you if you want it to. The good news about this is that it gives you hope! You can learn to cope

49

better and become stronger through your circumstances. You may not be able to control the events or circumstances in your life—those are considered uncontrollable because they are largely influenced by other people—but you can control your reactions to them![4]

This is why visualization and imagination are critical on the journey to achieving your goals. What you think about will become a part of you. What you choose to dwell on will be who you become. What do you want? Who do you want to become?

HOW TO NURTURE VISION

Find a picture that signifies your vision, and put it in front of you. When you see something long enough, it moves into your subconscious mind and eventually drops down into your spirit where you know that you know that it's going to happen. When you put a picture in front of you that represents your dream, you will begin to move toward your vision.

Post Your Dreams

When you see a picture of your vision, your vision can begin to increase. Something starts to take root inside of you that pulls you toward the action and essentially toward that vision. That's why putting a picture of your dream in front of you is a necessary step to attaining your goals.

A dream board, or vision board, is important to keep your goals visually in front of you. What it is, is a poster board or tack board, or something similar that you can use to post pictures symbolic of your goals and dreams. If you hang it in a high-traffic area of your house, you're bound to keep those dreams in front of you multiple times a day. There's something powerful about seeing them. It automatically makes you think about them, and what you see is what you get. Why? Your subconscious will act on what is seen.

I've heard it said that the refrigerator is magic. If you post a picture of something you want, you will more than likely get it. Now, it would be great if the refrigerator truly were a magical box, but it's not. It goes a bit deeper than that. The kitchen is a high-traffic area. The first thing I do when I enter the kitchen is to open the fridge and peer inside. I'm not sure what I'm looking for, but it's a habit I've created. Every time I go into the fridge, I see the picture I posted that symbolizes my dream, and it automatically helps me focus on my goal. It brings up emotions deep inside and makes me want to be better.

Doing this simple task will implant a picture in your mind of you obtaining that very goal. It is vital to visually keep your dreams and goals in front of you. As you focus on your goal, you will subconsciously do things to work toward that goal. Do you want to lose thirty pounds? Buy a cute outfit that's three sizes too small and stick it visibly in your closet so you see it every day as you are getting dressed. Do you want to finish your first marathon? Post a picture of the race course on your fridge. Do you want to get out of debt? Post a picture that symbolizes that very thing on your bathroom mirror. This begins to create a definiteness of purpose in your mind.

When Katy Perry was just nine years old, she made a vision board for a class project. Selena had just won a Grammy award that same year, 1993, and that is exactly what Perry chose to post on her board. She picked a photo of the famous Latin pop singer proudly holding her prized trophy and put the image in front of her. Wouldn't you know it, a short fifteen years later, Perry was nominated for her first Grammy Award, and she proudly accepted a beautiful golden statue that mirrored the one pictured in the photo she had taped onto her vision board back in grade school.[5]

While I was training to qualify for Boston, I made a 12x12 scrapbook page with my goal boldly written on it. On the page, I placed my time goal, a symbol of the Boston Marathon, and a map of the Boston race course. I developed this dream board with my goal attached. Then I hung it on my kitchen wall so I was forced to see it every time I walked by. I also had each of my kids create a picture for me that I hung by the garage door. Every time I walked out the door, it was a vivid reminder that my boys believed in me and that my dreams mattered.

At the Boston Marathon, I bought a shirt for my running friend who was training to qualify for the sought-after race as well. I gave it to her with the expectation that she would put it somewhere she could see it every day until she hit her goal and could proudly wear it. Which is exactly what she did. The day she put it on, I teared up knowing exactly what she had

51

been through to achieve her dream she had worked toward for years. I'm so glad I was able to experience that sweet victory with her.

Post images where you can see them. Create a dream board with pictures, words, symbols, or anything that will motivate you and inscribe a picture of your goal in your mind. Post them around the house. Create a dream scrapbook. Do what works for you, but don't skip this step. This physical reminder is an important step in becoming a visionary and keeping your goal directly in front of you.

This reminds me of Deuteronomy 11:18-19: "Fix these words of mine in your hearts and minds; tie them as symbols on your hands and bind them on your foreheads. Teach them to your children, talking about them when you sit at home and when you walk along the road, when you lie down and when you get up."

Whatever you put in front of you is what you will be drawn to. Whatever you talk about the most is what you will move toward. What do you want?

Preparation Is Key

While training, I watched the marathon course a few times a week. I was blessed that it was a major race, and an elite athlete had helped produce a short video of a car in fast forward driving through the actual course. She would highlight different spots along the way and share things one could expect throughout the course.

Not all marathons have that capability, but all have a course map. Visualizing it every week is vital for understanding how to train and what to expect. This leaves less room for surprises. You can see the elevation changes, the points that may be most challenging, and the water or food stops along the way.

Since there are many things beyond your control, preparation for anything in your control is crucial. There are two key factors that you have control over in any situation—your actions and your attitude. You can't control the weather, but you can control your attitude about the weather. You can't always control how you feel physically on race day, but you can control the action taken leading up to it. The idea of controlling that which you are able to will be developed more in chapter seven.

Dwell On It

I thought about my goal all the time. It was on my mind all day, every day. However, just because I thought about my goal all the time, doesn't mean I neglected all my daily responsibilities. There is a clear distinction between focus and obsession. You can make your goal a part of you and your everyday life without it becoming an unhealthy obsession. Don't get me wrong, you can't just visualize yourself into success without action, but action without vision is aimless.

Beyoncé, a renowned pop artist, set a picture of an Academy Award on the corner of her treadmill so she could use it as fuel to remind herself of her objective. She kept her goal in front of her, "She Put a Ring On It," and she took the time every day to dwell on the thing that she desired most. Not surprisingly, she was a star in the movie *Dream Girls*, which was nominated for an Academy Award.[7]

Wherever your focus is, that's what you'll concentrate on. For example, when you're looking at getting a new car, you love it, you buy it, and now it is everywhere you go. You see a plethora of people driving that style car. It's not that everyone went out and bought that same car when you did. It's just that your mind is focusing more on that specific car and picks it out on the road. Therefore, it seems like there are now a number of them around you.

My husband is a good example of this very thing, as he has a healthy obsession with Corvettes. That is his dream car, and he points them out everywhere he goes. He now even has my boys trained to holler, "Corvette!" whenever they see one pass by. Are there more Corvettes on the road than there were before it became his dream car? No, it's just that it's his favorite car and in the forefront of his mind. The mind is a powerful thing, and it can be trained to see and think the way we want it to.

Use Visualization

I had to think about my goal all the time. I needed to be single-minded and focus on that specific goal. I filtered all of my decisions based on if it would get me closer to my goal or further away. I chose not to get distracted. I chose to focus.

Visualization is crucial to any goal. Your goal needs to be at the forefront of your thoughts all the time. When you're thinking about your goal, you'll automatically start putting it first in your decision making, and the habits you create will line up with what you're trying to accomplish. Be willing to ask this question of any decision you make: "Will this get me closer to my goal, or will it hinder me from it?" Get good at putting your goal first. We'll talk quite a bit more about this in later chapters.

My oldest son is a junior elite men's gymnast, and he uses this tactic all the time. He finds other elite gymnasts who are a level ahead of him and watches their videos. He watches their technique and form. This creates a desire in him to perform at his best. He sees himself hitting every routine every time.

He really enjoyed watching the national champion a level ahead of him because he knew his performances were fairly flawless. He knew that watching him wouldn't hinder his training, but, rather, it would enhance it. He became virtual friends with the other gymnast, and eventually, they met at a national event and became real life friends.

Now, what's even more special about this story is that my husband actually met the family first while on a work trip. There, the nationally-ranked gymnast gave him a gift to bring home to my son. It was a "ship in a bottle", but instead of a ship, the bottle was filled with men's gymnastics apparatuses. His grandpa had built it for him. This gift was a symbol of a friendship that was about to flourish, but my son also put it on the shelf as a reminder of what he really wants. He uses it to drive himself to the next level.

I'm amazed at how much time my son takes to visualize where he is and where he wants to be. If given a choice between watching gymnastics and watching a movie, he'd choose gymnastics 90 percent of the time.

EMOTIONALIZE YOUR VISION

Say it, see it, and achieve it. We first need to speak what it is we want, and we have to put in the effort and work to achieve it. But the middle part is just as important—seeing it. It goes deeper than visualizing it all the time. The goal actually needs to seep so far down inside of you that it draws out emotion. Can you see yourself at the end of your goal? Can you see yourself at the finish line? What does it look like? How does it make you feel? What's going on in your mind at that point? Do you see it? Do you really see it? Emotionalize your vision.

Picture It Already Done

Another important factor in visualization is picturing what it will be like when you accomplish your goal. Close your eyes and see yourself at that place. For me, I envisioned myself at the finish line with three hours and thirty minutes on the clock. I didn't just visualize that once. It was a daily occurrence.

I also visualized "3:30" on the clock at the finish of every training run. I imagined what it would be like crossing the finish line at three hours and thirty minutes. I became emotional just thinking about it. I saw my eyes welling up and would sometimes shed actual tears of joy thinking about it—it felt so real. It burned a picture in my mind because I envisioned it enough times, and I believed it was already done.

Because I had learned to see myself where I wanted to be, I went into race day with a confidence I probably wouldn't have had otherwise. I wasn't surprised when I crossed the finish line with "3:30:06" blaring back at me in bright red lettering. I had seen that goal as already accomplished before I even began the race.

Visualization is critical in accomplishing any dream. You have to see it in your mind before it manifests. You have to believe it before you see it. Whether you believe you can accomplish your goal or whether you don't believe you can do it, you're right. You can be your strongest proponent, but you can also be your strongest opponent. All self-doubt needs to be banished. It has no place in your life.

Faith needs to be cultivated like a farmer cultivating a field. No farmer says to himself, "I'll plant these seeds, but I fear they won't produce." No, a farmer plants his seeds expecting a harvest in the fall. I plant my seed by making a definite decision, then I cultivate it through my training with full expectation that it will be fruitful.

Faith and fear cannot coexist. Faith trumps self-doubt. Now, realistically, you can never truly banish self-doubt, but you can discover ways to overcome it and fight it when it does creep in. You can create enough self-belief that when the doubt attempts to overtake you, you are prepared to overcome it. A key component in this is to visualize your goal, because the more real it is to you, the more faith you will have in the desired outcome.

Don't Limit Yourself

Don't limit yourself with your own imagination. Don't say, "I can't imagine ever writing a book." "I can't imagine ever completing a marathon." "I can't imagine starting my own business." "I can't imagine _____." Don't limit yourself. Don't let the enemy come and steal your dream because your imagination is limited. God's dream for your life is even bigger than your own dream. His ways are higher than our ways. You need to use your imagination to see your vision to fruition. You need to see yourself at the finish of the race. Use that imagination. Use it to your benefit.

You need to see yourself finishing your race with a personal best time. You need to see yourself living in your dream house. You need to see yourself thirty pounds lighter. You need to see your bank account growing. Your imagination is like a muscle, you need to work with it every day. Before you go to bed, or when you wake up, find a comfy chair or a cozy corner and sit with your own thoughts in the quiet, imagining your future. Start with just a few minutes a day. The more you imagine, the larger your vision expands.

SHARE YOUR VISION

It is easy to let ourselves down, but we'll fight harder not to let others down. Sharing our vision creates an urgency for us to actually finish what we say we are going to do. Community is a powerful force, so let it work for you. Share your vision with those who will challenge or stretch you to pursue it.

Accountability

If you share your plan with people you trust, they can hold you accountable to moving forward. Give them permission to ask you the tough questions. Are you creating habits in your life that will get you where you want to go? How are your daily disciplines going? Do you think you should do less of ...? Do you think you should do more of ...? Having someone willing to speak into your life is important as you reach for your goals. That person can help keep you on track. That person can motivate you. That person can become your biggest cheerleader.

Consider finding a coach. Are you trying to hit a specific marathon time? A running coach can help you plan your trainings and give you insights you may not otherwise see. Do you have mental blocks preventing you from moving forward? Consider hiring a mental training coach who can help you work through those mind barriers. Do you want to lose weight? Consider hiring a health coach who can give you specific fitness and meal plans. Do you want to start a business? Consider hiring a business consultant who can help you get started. On our own, we may not be willing to stick to the disciplines required by each of these goals, but when we invest in these areas, we are more likely to be more serious and follow through.

Be Bold

Declare your vision. Shout it from the mountaintops!!! Okay, I'm kind of kidding around, but if you do live in the mountains, why not? Express your excitement for what lies ahead. If you're not willing to be bold about your goals, you are likely going to quit on yourself.

When you share your vision with others, it solidifies and deepens your commitment to finish. If you don't follow through after declaring your goal, people will know. It creates a positive peer pressure and an unspoken accountability to yourself. You've declared it, so now you need to do it.

"See, the former things have taken place, and new things I declare; before they spring into being, I announce them to you." (Isaiah 42:9)

Speaking your goals out loud before you know how they will come to be or see any results is a key ingredient in the success factor. Saying it is a huge part of seeing it. The more you hear it, the more you will believe it. The more you believe it, the more you will act on it. It creates a larger vision of the goal at hand. Once it's said, it's hard to take back. You have now, out loud, solidified what you plan to do.

Involve Your Family

My boys were an inspiration to me. They believed in me so much that I couldn't just give up on myself. Including your kids in your dreams helps to teach them the principles of success. My boys made dream posters for me to motivate me and keep me going when I doubted myself. We posted them right by our garage entry so I could see them each time we left the house. Because I included my boys in the process, I had an extra level of accountability to get the job done. I didn't want to let them down. I now felt that, not only was I doing this for me, but I was also doing this for them.

A dear running friend's son made a blue and yellow bracelet for her when she was in the midst of her training to qualify for the Boston Marathon. Blue and yellow are the symbolic colors of the cherished race. She didn't ask him to make it for her, he just did it. Her training and goal-setting were inspirational to him, and by making the bracelet for her, he was not only telling her he believed in her, but more importantly, he was telling her that he was watching her. Her going after her goal would inspire him and show him he can go after his own dreams.

It's easy to use family as an excuse not to do something. We can hide behind our daily responsibilities and our parenting and easily miss out on what God is trying to teach us. He can use our goals and dreams to inspire others, to help us grow ourselves, and to press into Him. Our goals could ultimately be what's best for our family. Our children will rise to the level we set for them. What better way is there to teach them how to do hard things than simply doing hard things ourselves?

I want my boys to see me striving for something more. I want them to learn how to succeed from me. I want them to know that when they grow up and have a family of their own, their dreams still matter. So often we drop our own dreams by the wayside in declaration that it's best for our families. What's best for your family is for them to see achievement and a purposeful life from you! Become your children's best example. You fight the good fight.

Why is it okay for us to not go after something but yet expect our kids to? Who are they going to learn it from otherwise? Success breeds success. Show them what that looks like. Model accomplishment and a no-quit attitude for them. This is an important point, and maybe even more crucial in the teenage years when they are trying to figure out who they are and what they are meant to do. They will look up to someone. The question is, do you want it to be an entertainer, athlete, peer, or do you want it to be you?

Kids need to learn how to set and maintain goals too. For a while, our family goal was to get me out of my full-time job so I could come home and take care of our family. My boys knew this was a top priority for us at the time. We talked to them about it every day, and it got to the point where leaving my job became as much of an objective for them as it was for me. My oldest would randomly yell, "Mommy freedom!" It was cute, but it also served its motivational purpose.

One day as I was getting ready for work, my oldest son said to me, "Where are you going?" I told him I had to go to work, so he had to go to grandpa's house, and as much as he loves grandpa and grandma, I saw disappointment written all over his face. He said to me, "I want you free with me. I don't like it when you go to work. It makes me sad." If that's not motivation, I don't know what is.

Your kids will motivate you to grow if you allow them to be a part of your goals. I couldn't give up on that dream because my boys were counting on me to achieve it. I would have let them down, too, if I quit pursuing freedom, and it would have given them a reason to be able to quit on their own dreams. I wasn't going to let that happen. I strive to be their first example.

The day I left my full-time job, we all felt the sweet victory. Each of us knew what it took to get us to a place where we could make it happen. We all sacrificed our time to see it come to fruition. We all won that day. We all felt the triumph that comes with having a goal and crushing it.

Our children can be our best motivators if we let them. Allowing them to participate in our success as we pursue the dream in our hearts shows them the greatest example we can model. It gives them the go-ahead to dream, to achieve, to be great. I never want to be their excuse for giving up. I also never want them to think that when they have a family they have to stop dreaming. I don't want them to give up on improving their fitness or pushing themselves to their full potential. Continual growth is crucial. Growth doesn't end after high school or college. It is a constant objective for the rest of our lives. We are either growing, or we are dying. Which do you choose to be doing?

FINAL STRETCH

Walt Disney had a clear picture of his vision, it was burned into his mind, and he was able to clearly communicate that vision to others. Disney World's grand opening in 1971 happened five years AFTER the great visionary Walt Disney passed away. During the dedication ceremony, someone asked his wife, "Isn't it a shame that Walt didn't live to see this?" Mrs. Disney responded with, "He did see it, that's why it's here."[8]

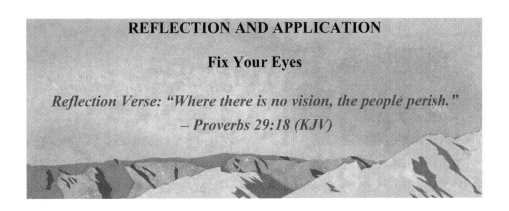

God places desires in our heart, and it's our duty to go to work and bring those desires into fruition. The gifts we have are meant to enable us to fulfill our calling and purpose. It is our duty to carry out the vision set forth in front of us. Psalm 37:4-5 says, "Take delight in the Lord, and He will give you the desires of your heart." Delight means "to take pleasure in." We can't take pleasure in someone we don't know. In order for God to stir up desires in our hearts, we need to spend time in fellowship with him. Godly desires are birthed in prayer. Mark 11:24 says, "Whatever you ask for in prayer, believe that you have received it, and it will be yours." Do not let the thought of failure keep you from stepping out and pursuing the desire of your heart—your calling. As the desires are being stirred in your heart, allow God to give you a clear vision as to how they will come to pass.

Reflection Questions:

1. What is one thing you need to start doing to make time for your goal?

2. What is one thing you can quit doing to make time for your goal?

3. How can you make your family a priority while pursuing your passions?

4. Is there someone you can ask to hold you accountable as you pursue your goals?

5. As you spend time in the word and prayer, take note of the desires that are stirring up. Have you already identified any? If so, what are they?

Further Reading:

- Ephesians 1:17-18

- 2 Corinthians 4:18

- Philippians 4:8-9

Application: Create your own dream board, post it in a visible location, look at it multiple times a day, and visualize your dreams coming to pass.

Materials needed:

- Poster board, 12x12 cardstock, pin board, etc.
- Magazines or printed pictures
- Words to inspire/quotes to go along with your goal
- Glue/tape/tacks

BE CREATIVE! HAVE FUN WITH IT!

Chapter 5

Create Your Race Plan

"By failing to prepare, you are preparing to fail."
– Benjamin Franklin

Chess is a game of strategy and persistence. In order to be effective, players need to know what each piece is able to do and also need to logically create a game plan against their opponents. My boys love the game of chess. They know all the rules and moves in the game, but they still lose to their dad every time. Why? My husband's an average chess player, but the advantage he has over the boys is that he plans three to four moves in advance.

A chess master not only plans three to four moves ahead, but he also has moves planned for many possible scenarios in response to what his opponent may do. It is a mind game. Advanced players formulate mini game plans in their minds. They draft a Plan A, Plan B, and so forth.

The game of life is similar. Like chess, we need to develop a strategy for the vision we set in front of ourselves. We need to know the role of each piece, such as our skills, gifts, and talents. These could also be the people we have surrounding us and the resources we have allotted to us.

Once we know the pieces we have to work with, we can formulate a plan, or plans, to effectively advance toward our dreams. We can lay out a strategy toward one goal, which will lead us to the next, and continue in a stepping stone manner until we are the victors of our vision. "Goals in writing are dreams with deadlines," says motivational speaker and author Brian Tracy. A game plan begins with a decision, but it is backed by action and a plan. Without those two ingredients, a decision is merely a wish.

63

PLAN VS. NO PLAN

In order to know where you are going, it is extremely important to have a game plan. When you have a plan, you have a clear direction. You are more easily able to see the action steps necessary to obtain your objective. A plan keeps you focused on the main purpose and keeps you on track. Without a thought out plan, you essentially lose the road map that will guide you along the path to successfully accomplishing your dream.

Lessons Learned

Marathon #1: *My first race was all about finishing with no other expectations attached.* I had just had my second baby boy, and I decided it would be a great idea to run a half marathon to get back into shape. Six months after having him, that's exactly what I did. The half was exhilarating, and I craved more. I was already halfway there, so I thought, why not? I trained to run a full marathon just three months later. My training plan consisted of something I found online that looked appealing. I was training to run with no goals and no preconceived notions. I finished at a respectable four hours and twelve minutes. Race day came and went, and I still craved more. Since I had accomplished the first milestone, I could expand my dream. My first real goal seemed lofty—qualify for the Boston Marathon.

Marathon #2: *I had the goal to qualify, but I didn't have a specific game plan. I just trained and ran. I had little direction.* I trained very similar to marathon number one. I picked a training plan online and went to work. I needed to cut thirty-seven minutes off my finish time. I didn't really do anything differently this time around other than pick a goal. Isn't it funny, that my finish time of four hours and ten minutes was similar to my first race!

Marathon #3: *I had a game plan and a coach.* I decided it was time to have a coach who could be objective and challenge me. I trained with a group at a local fitness club, and they quickly became my workout family. Our trainer was knowledgeable and knew how to push me closer to my limit. I used a new training plan and incorporated speed intervals and hill training, something I was lacking in the first two races. This time, I ended up slightly closer to my goal with a finish time of three hours and fifty-one minutes. This was at Grandma's Marathon, and I was incredibly proud of cutting nineteen minutes from my previous marathon. However, as you know, I still had sixteen minutes to shave.

Marathon #4: *I had a game plan and backed it up with expectation and mental training.* This one was different. Before I signed up for the race, I made the decision to do whatever it took. I was decided. I followed a very specific training plan. I cleaned up my diet and added in a strict weights program to increase strength. However, the most significant difference was applying all the success principles I had been learning up to that point. I created a clear vision of what I wanted and put pictures in front of me. I wrote down my specific goal with affirmations to speak. My focus was un-interrupted. If you asked me if I would do it, I would have told you emphatically, "Yes!" I felt it. I believed it with every fiber of my being, and this was the race that defined me. I crushed my goal of three hours and thirty minutes through pain and tears, but I did it with a clear vision and the action to back it up. The difference maker was that I had a specific game plan supported by action and belief.

Importance of The Game Plan

Having a plan is the key to accomplishing any goal. A game plan is a pre-worked strategy that you use to attain your goal. It helps you to think, strategize, and lay out what it will take to move on. It becomes a road map for you to use as you take action in pursuit of your dream. Ensuring you have a specified plan put in place is vital for three reasons:

1. A game plan aids in discipline. Being disciplined in one area helps you become disciplined in all areas. The more disciplined you are, the easier it is to get rid of the habit of procrastination. Discipline moves you past wanting to wait and instills a healthy proactivity to get the job done.

2. A game plan gives you focus. You become less distractible. Distractions lose their stronghold on you, and it's easier to decipher the good from the best. When you become decided, many

"opportunities" may come your way, but focus helps you to filter them—will they get you closer to your goal or hinder it?

3. A game plan gives you purpose. It gives you motivation to keep going. You've set a finish point and are excited to see it come to completion. It helps you to live life on purpose. You're excited to get out of bed every day because you're in pursuit of greatness. You now have something to strive for.

What Happens Without A Plan

In the fall of 2017, the year after my first Boston Marathon, I chose to run the Marine Corps Marathon in Washington D.C. We formed a family vacation around that race. My plan was to have no plan. At the time, I thought this was a brilliant idea! I had run multiple marathons and was confident in my ability. I trained for mileage, but I didn't have a specific time goal or training plan. I felt fairly healthy since I wasn't training hard, so I was hopeful for a solid race.

Race day came, and I ran with no expectations, no mental training, and no wrist watch. Not wearing a watch meant I couldn't track my pace, my overall time, or my heart rate. I had nothing tangible to evaluate my progress and had to depend solely on how I felt to get me through. I even ran without my music for the first eighteen miles just to see how far I could go without it.

The Marine Corps Marathon is known for its scenic route through the National Mall and finishes at the Marine Corps War Memorial. The most emotional part of the course, around the halfway point, is the "Wear Blue Mile" where American flags and pictures of fallen service members decorate the roadway. I consider it the mile of silence because not a word is uttered throughout the memorial to these fallen heroes. With all these moments to look forward to, I just wanted to enjoy the experience and take it all in.

I started out too fast—first mistake. What I quickly realized was that, even though I wanted a casual race without pressures, no plan was ultimately a bad choice. I didn't have a plan for time, so I ran quicker than

I should have. Without a watch, I couldn't really tell how fast I was running, I just knew it was probably too fast. I didn't have a plan in place if an issue arose, and, of course, problems arose! Not only did I have bathroom issues, but my right leg went completely numb, which made for a miserable final eight miles. I walked more in that race than I ever have before.

That race, though a memorable experience, was the worst I've ever had and made me doubt my future in racing. Working without a plan creates roadblocks that could otherwise be avoided. No plan means no vision. No vision means no direction. No direction means no discipline. No discipline means mediocre training. A plan is necessary to hit a desired outcome.

THE FRAMEWORK OF A GAME PLAN

There are a few key ingredients to a solid game plan. It starts with defining your dream and ends when you achieve it. A game plan then is broken down into smaller, attainable goals. Each goal is a checkpoint along the race course toward your dream. With any goal, you need a specified deadline, actionable tasks, and flexibility for adjustments.

Be Purposeful And Know Your Why

Work toward doing things on purpose and with a purpose. You have to know the "why" behind what you're doing. Your WHY is the most important part. If you don't have a why, you won't succeed. What is a why? Your WHY is something that is so strong that it eventually becomes a need. It may have started as a want, but once it's been burned it into your imagination, it becomes a need, a must have. Your WHY needs to be something you've deemed significant enough that you can't live without it. Your WHY will get your butt off the couch and out the door every day. Your WHY is worth fighting for. Your WHY will jolt you out of bed in the morning.

You might say, "I want to lose 50 pounds." But why? Maybe it's because you want to be healthy and active with your kids and see them grow up. You might say, "I want to start my own business." But why?

Maybe it's because you don't want to live paycheck to paycheck anymore. You want to live on your own terms, not be capped by income, and not have to ask for time off. You could say, "I want to win the championship game." But why? Maybe it's because it gives you a larger platform of influence so you can affect the cause most passionate to your heart.

It may take time to find your true, actual why. It may not be the first thing you think of. It may not even be your initial why because the *real* why has to be deep enough to drive you to do the work. Your why can evolve over time. It has to motivate you to keep going when the going gets tough. Not just anything will do that. You may need to spend quite a bit of time reflecting and cultivating your why. A good time to do this is in the morning when you first wake up. Find a spot to be still and take the time to think. Think about what it is you want, and reflect on the "why" behind it. Journal your thoughts. Develop them each day as you look back on what you wrote.

My why was to be an example for my kids but also to prove to myself that I was capable of doing hard things. I wanted to see just how far I could take myself out of my comfort zone. I wanted to see if the success principles I had been learning actually worked. I wanted to do something of significance. Maybe your why is financial, maybe it's for your family, or maybe it's for freedom. Maybe you want to start your own business so you can be your own boss. Maybe you want to get out of debt so you can experience financial freedom. Whatever your why is, you need to make sure that it becomes emotional to you.

Knowing your why helps you to filter your daily decisions and stay focused. Your why is a purpose, cause, or belief that inspires you and makes you want to become better. Your why fuels your drive and desire.

Having a purpose is powerful. Your why is your purpose, and, with it, comes singleness of purpose. Without purpose you will go about your day doing things without really understanding why you are doing them. Purpose creates order and discipline. Purpose drives a plan. Having chaos in your life is optional, and purpose prevents chaos.

Goals Equal Baby Steps Toward Your Dream

A dream is a larger, long-term goal or vision for your life. Goals are shorter-term stepping stones necessary along the long-term journey. It's these smaller, incremental goals that set you up to attain your dream. We laid out how to develop a dream in chapter three. Goals are a part of your game plan to lead you to your dream.

Think of goals as baby steps. When walking around on a daily basis, what's easier? Taking small, consistent steps or striding out as far as you can go? You may think you'll get to your destination more quickly with exaggerated strides, but you'll actually tire faster. If you set smaller goals and think of them as baby steps, you'll be less likely to give up.

Smaller, more achievable goals will help you feel accomplished and measure results more quickly. If you're only looking to the long-term dream, it will feel so far removed that you will get discouraged easily and lose motivation. Think baby steps!

Have you heard people say things like, "They got lucky," or, "The cards were dealt in their favor?" The reason they say that is because many successful people appear to have "made it" overnight. The truth to this, though, is that it actually took years of working toward their goals with their daily habits to get them to where they are. It's in the behind the scenes, what they do when no one is looking, where they actually succeeded. They were willing to be consistent and persistent long enough to "make it" and appear as though it was an overnight success.

This is like the basketball player who shoots hundreds of free throws after the rest of the team called it a night. It's the wrestler who chose to run stairs in the early morning before any of his teammates arrived. It's the kicker who practices extra hours when the rest of the team is partying. It's the goalie who comes in early and stands in front of the net having hundreds of pucks hit at him in attempts to deflect a goal. The "overnight success" happens through consistent, daily habits that don't seem like they make a huge difference, but strung together over time, they are monumental and game changers.

DEFINE YOUR GAME PLAN

We're limited to our current knowledge, so in devising your game plan, it may be wise to seek advice from a coach or mentor who can help you define the right game plan for you. They will look at it from an unemotional perspective and be able to see things you can't see about yourself. Your coach will be able to give you a specific route to follow and help you see what you may need to change along the way.

Three Main Steps

How do you draft a game plan? What are the necessary ingredients that go into it? There are three key steps to your game plan, and each is equal in importance. You need to define what the successful result of the goal looks like, define when you want the desired result, and define the initial actions you believe are the best to take in moving toward that result.

1. Define the goal. Write it out. Make it realistic but also a little challenging, something that will stretch you. You will not fight for something that is too easy, but you also want it to be believable to you. A goal is essentially a dream, or a stepping stone to fulfill that dream, but the difference is that it has a plan attached. Without a plan, it is merely a wish. I want you to dream a dream larger than yourself, and then we will break it down into smaller, more manageable chunks. You need to commit to working toward one dream, or vision, at a time, but you may have a few goals intermixed en route to the desired result.

2. Define a deadline. Without a deadline, you don't have a truly clear direction. Without clear direction, you will not stick to your goal. Without clear direction, there is an underlying component of aimlessness. According to Napoleon Hill, the most important thing to have is a "definiteness of purpose," which means knowing exactly what you want, knowing exactly when you want it, and knowing exactly what you are willing to give up to get it.[1]

3. Create a written plan. This may look differently based on the person and the goal, but one thing is for sure, writing it down is a secret ingredient. Habakkuk 2:2 says, "Write the vision and make it plain." Know what you want and how you will get there, and know it in writing. Ask yourself some key questions. What do I need to do every day to hit my deadline? What is most important? How do I prioritize my responsibilities? What habits do I need to develop to see this plan through? Am I focusing on only one goal, or do I need to focus on a few smaller goals related to the larger vision? Is my written plan a daily, weekly, or monthly plan— maybe it's all of those?

Following these three main steps will help you turn your dream into a game plan. You can be flexible as you live out the plan, but without something written down it will be difficult to bring your dreams to fruition.

Do Something With It

Take action. It's important to do something every day toward your goal. This is the same concept of compounding interest. Doing little things every day toward your goal may not seem to make a difference, but in the long run, it's monumental in accomplishing what you set out to do. You're not even capable of learning until you're in motion. If you have a coach, he can't help you unless you're in the midst of your battle, so get in the fight!

It's easier to take small steps at a time, things that seem easy, rather than long jump after long jump after long jump, which will lead to burnout. If you take small steps and accomplish little goals along the way, it's easier to track progress and keep moving forward to the larger goal at hand. Plus, achieving even smaller things will encourage you to take the next steps. What is better, working out for an hour a day, five days a week, or five straight hours on Saturday? Take action each day to get closer to your goal.

Willingness To Sacrifice

With every goal, there comes a sacrifice. If your goal is to run a marathon, you may have to give up sleep or TV time to get that long run

71

in on the weekend. If you want something to change in your life, you're going to have to make small sacrifices. Nothing changes until something changes—profound, I know. If you claim you want to lose ten pounds, but you continue to have that bowl of ice cream before bed, are you going to lose those ten pounds? No, because nothing changed.

EVALUATE AND ADJUST

Just as important as setting the game plan is evaluating what's working, and adjusting any key areas that seem to be off. The path may change. You may set up a game plan and realize something isn't effective. You may need to tweak a few things and see if that helps. Work the plan, evaluate, adjust if necessary, and continue plowing ahead toward the goal.

Specific Week-To-Week And Day-To-Day Plans

Goals are not achieved overnight. They are achieved one day at a time. Each night, plan what you will do the next day to move closer to your goal. I do this with running. Sunday evening I schedule my week of workouts and when I will be able to fit them all in. I treat them like an appointment. Because they are in my calendar, I am better able to stick to the plan. It feels important, so I treat it as a priority.

Sometimes my plans change, and sometimes I need to be flexible, but I work hard to keep my schedule as best as possible. Some may say it's extreme to schedule a workout, but I would say scheduling my health is of utmost importance. If I don't schedule it, it may not happen. It may get pushed aside for other things that demand my attention. I'm no good to anyone else unless I am healthy.

Create a daily morning routine. Decide what time you will get up in the morning, and decide on three to five non-negotiables that you will get done before your day begins. Consistency is key to creating good habits. I wake up around the same time every day, even on the weekends, and I have my quiet time, read a personal development book, journal my thoughts, speak my affirmations, and workout.

My days feel off when I don't make time for my daily routine. It rejuvenates me and gets me ready to tackle the projects or the obstacles I may face. I'm also more productive, and my creativity heightens when I stick to these non-negotiables. My energy levels are higher on days when I make an effort to complete my morning routine.

Not a morning person? No problem, you have a couple of choices. Become one, or choose to do an evening routine before bed. If I try to read before bed, I don't get anything out of it because I'm drifting off to sleep. However, if that's not you, and you do your best work late at night, don't think you have to become a morning person to be effective at creating your daily habits. If you're willing to be persistent and consistent, then morning, afternoon, or evening will do.

Track Progress

Tracking your progress is the secret ingredient to the game plan, and this is one step most people skip! The reason? They've already quit. It's best to not continually check for results because results don't usually show up overnight and may be hard to see, but it's also important to keep a record of how things are working for you within your specific game plan.

We live in a world with a microwave mentality, which means we want quick fixes, so we rush from one thing to the next. When it comes to goals, we need to think of them like an oven. It takes time to preheat (gain momentum). It takes time to cook (take consistent action). It takes time to cool (hit our goal). There is no shortcut to working the plan other than knowing that every little thing you do for your goal matters.

Successful people normally do not hit their goals with Plan A. Unsuccessful people quit after Plan A doesn't pan out. Fear of failure in action. Successful people plow on into Plan B, Plan C, and so on. Sometimes it takes until Plan Z to finally get the results they are looking for. The point is, they persevere and don't quit at the sight of the first obstacle.

Thomas Edison, well-known inventor of the light bulb, understood this principle all too well. Edison made more than one thousand unsuccessful attempts of inventing the light bulb, but that didn't seem to phase him. He just kept on persisting. When asked about it, he simply replied, "I didn't fail 10,000 times. I've just found 10,000 ways that won't work." He went on to say, "Many of life's failures are people who did not realize how close they were to success when they gave up."[2]

Track your progress so you can identify what is and isn't working, but continue to move forward. Look for results, but choose not to measure results too early. Stay consistent and persistent.

Make Adjustments

It's fine to improvise your schedule at times when life happens, because it will. But it's also important to discipline your flesh and create new habits. What in the world does that mean? Your "flesh" is your feelings. Your flesh may not want to be put in a hard situation. Your flesh may not want to put in the work. Your flesh may want to sit on the couch with a bag of potato chips and just be pure lazy. Doing things when you just don't feel like it is paramount to overcoming your flesh.

Overcoming your flesh means you aren't easily swayed by your emotions. It means you don't cave at every temptation. It means you hold strong to doing what you say you're going to do. When life happens, and you're not just making excuses, ask yourself these adjustment questions:

- What's working? Why?
- What's not working? Why?
- What are you willing to add?
- What are you willing to give up?
- What are you willing to invest?
- Can you see the adjustments you need to make?
- Can you make those necessary adjustments?

Once you're in motion, doing the work of the game plan, you are ready to make adjustments if necessary. Your coach can help you see what's working and what still needs to be tweaked.

IMPORTANCE OF COMMUNITY

When at least two crabs are put into a bucket, they can't escape. Why? When one tries to claw its way out, the other pulls it right back into captivity. Beware! This happens to dreamers too when they surround themselves with negative people. One thing I encourage you to do is to associate with people who have what you want. Do you want a great marriage? Hang out with couples who have a great marriage. Do you want to be healthy? Hang out with someone who has her nutrition in check. Do you want to be wealthy? Hang out with someone who is financially sound. Community is key.

Association

Choosing whom you associate with can make or break your success. Consider this. Your friend is negative about the dream you have set forth in front of you. He ridicules it and makes fun of you for it. He doesn't have big dreams. He pressures you to go out partying with him after work instead of encouraging you to pursue the vision you have for your life.

Now, pretend you are standing on a chair, and your friend is on the ground. You both have a grasp of each other's hand. You are trying to pull him up to your level while he is trying to pull you down to his. Which is easier? It would be easier for your friend to pull you down off the chair than it would be for you to pull your friend up with you—the law of gravity at work. That's the power of association.

You may think that continuing to associate with him will be beneficial because he may change, but in all actuality, if you hang out with a negative person, he will eventually drag you down with him. You need to carefully choose whom you spend your time with. Will that person try to pull you down, or are they standing on the chair, side by side with you, cheering you on and maybe even stepping in the race with you?

Cheerleaders

A cheerleader is someone who is always in your corner encouraging you. No matter how hard you are on yourself, no matter how many times you fail, a cheerleader will build up your confidence with encouraging words and unconditional support.

When my friend, Kristen, was at the twenty-four mile marker, cheering her head off for me, it was exactly what I needed—that extra nudge to keep me going toward my goal. She was there at the exact moment I felt like giving up. The moment the negative was beginning to consume my thoughts.

Steer clear from naysayers! Negative people may seem fine in the moment, but you always feel worse after associating with them. Cheerleaders, on the other hand, make you feel better about yourself after you've spent time with them.

On the other hand, what do you do if you can't get away from a negative person because it's a close family member, or even a spouse? It's important to share your dreams and goals with those closest to you, but if your mom or dad or spouse or whoever is really not supportive of your passions, it can be a really hard place to be.

If you are in that situation, I encourage you to reach out to one or two friends close to you who are supportive and can be cheerleaders for you. Ask them to be your rock in this season. Be willing to be open and vulnerable with them. When negativity comes from the unsupportive loved one, those friends can help lift you up and keep you going. They become like family because you are stretched to be on a deeper level of trust with them.

Share less with the unsupportive loved one than you would with others who are more positive. If all they will do is complain or tell you that your goals don't matter, then it's better to change the subject all together. Keep those conversations for your friends who are your rock.

I know this is easy to say and hard to do, but if you keep steady in pursuing your goals, your loved ones may change their tune and slowly start making positive comments or even changing things about their own pursuits. And they may not. But you can't let that keep you from doing what you know in your heart of hearts you are called to do. Lean on one or two close friends to get you through.

Accountability And Shared Goals

I used to be a lone runner. I did it all on my own—my motivation, my runs, my support. It wasn't until I became a part of a running group, that I realized community was a missing link I didn't even know I needed.

I was encouraged to check out Moms on the Run when I began my journey as a running coach. Moms on the Run is a nationally recognized fitness program for women of all ages and fitness levels, not just moms. Their mission is to "inspire and transform women through a healthy lifestyle of fitness, fun, and friendship."[3] That appealed to me, so I went for it.

What I found is a group of women who wanted to grow together. They hold each other accountable to be where they say they're going to be when they say they're going to be there and do what they say they're going to do. They laugh with each other, cry with each other, and hold each other up.

When you find a group of people that are going in the same direction with similar visions, something magical happens. You create a network of supporters. You create positive peer pressure. You find accountability. You find your tribe.

I found my tribe with Moms on the Run, and I love that not only am I coaching these women toward their fitness goals, but they are inspiring me daily to become better as well. They hold me accountable to be the best version of myself that I can be.

This is the same in the race of life! Finding your tribe, a group of like-minded people who are running the same race, keeps you healthier, happier, and motivated. These individuals can stretch you to reach the next level. When you are surrounded by others who aren't willing to compromise and are going all in with something, it's hard not to get on the bandwagon and keep moving forward.

What tribe are you looking for? A tribe of business owners? A tribe of mothers? A tribe of athletes? A tribe of dreamers? I've realized through this journey that I couldn't have done it alone. I can't be successful without people who build my confidence and uplift me. Neither can you.

The Value Of A Coach Or Mentor

Find people in life, who are where you want to be, and learn from them. Friends who haven't done what you are trying to accomplish can be an encouragement to you. They can support you, but they can't give you the mentorship you need. Take advice from those who have gone before you because they know how to get where you want to go.

A mentor has been there and done that. You can learn from his experience. He can take you on a journey as you discover who you are. The main difference between a cheerleader and a mentor is that a cheerleader is an uplifter looking for all the positives, but a mentor is willing to go deeper and share hard truths with you when you need them and, many times, when you don't want to hear them.

A mentor is someone you allow to speak into your life. You are willing to become vulnerable with this person so he can invoke truth and wisdom into your game plan. Mentors are able to see things you may not be able to. Their past experiences allow them to see the situation from an alternate angle. Mentors can help you tweak your game plan when it doesn't seem to be working.

Who are you taking advice from? Do you have someone speaking into your life? Do you need to find a mentor or a coach? Are you willing to be vulnerable to another person?

Keeping Family First

When I say prioritize your goal, it doesn't mean let that goal come between you and your family. Our lives shouldn't be consumed with kids and their activities alone. Our kids also need to fit into our goals. They are a part of God's plan for our lives. He casts a vision for us, and our kids are a part of that greater vision. Make sure your personal goal lines up with your family goal. Keep your family first, which is sometimes easier said than done. Don't let daily responsibilities slip. Take pride in all you do, but in order to achieve the goal, there will be a period of time where you will have to sacrifice something. It may be sleep, entertainment, or fewer social engagements, but it should never be at your family's expense.

Taking Sunday afternoon for my long training runs was taxing on both me and my family. It was a three– to five–hour stint. Because of this, I made sure my other training runs didn't affect our family flow. I would get up earlier and run before my kids were awake and my husband left for work. Or, we would go to the YMCA for a break mid-day. The boys could play or swim, and I could get my workout in. On Sunday nights I would pull out my schedule and see where I could fit in my runs. I'd schedule them like an appointment. I would prioritize my week, but it was important to leave room for my workouts or "me" time.

To keep family first, you need to get good at prioritizing and scheduling. We didn't make every play date or family get together. We didn't do extra activities. We tried to keep things simple during the stint of me accomplishing my dream. I was still working and running kids around to activities, but we did cut what we could when we could.

It was important for me to pick and choose what we did so that anytime we were together could be quality time, and I could be present. I worked to not only be there with my kids but to be present for my kids. Those are two totally different things. Being there is a task, or a responsibility. Being present is about making the most of that time, building up my kids, encouraging them, playing with them, and enjoying them.

Because I let my family in on my goals, they were just as excited about them as I was. They wanted me to succeed, and that made my long Sunday runs and other parts of my training easier to handle. Let your family in on your goals. Let them be your cheerleaders and support. It won't always be easy, but as long as you allow them to see the vision, you will persevere.

FINAL STRETCH

People don't succeed by chance. It's not chance, it's a choice. It starts with a decision, then a plan, and finally, working the plan while tracking progress and making adjustments as necessary. What is your game plan? Do you have a better idea of how to create one now? Do you need a coach or mentor to help you build a specific plan? Do you need to set some smaller goals along the way? Let's recap the main steps in our game planning process:

1. Define the goal in writing
2. Define a definite deadline
3. Create a written plan
4. Take action
5. Evaluate and adjust
6. Associate
7. See it through

"Plan your work, and work your plan." – Margaret Thatcher

Importance of One Degree

Reflection Verse: "'For I know the plans I have for you,'
declares the Lord. 'Plans to prosper you and not to harm you,
plans to give you hope and a future.'"
– Jeremiah 29:11

The game plan is where God's purpose and our passion meet. It is an extremely important piece of the puzzle. The game plan sets you up for success. It's your road map to fulfill your calling. I remember growing up hearing an analogy of how important it is for a pilot to stay on course. If an airplane is even one degree off course, it can set the pilot up for failure and land him in a totally different destination.

If a pilot is just one degree off course:

- For every degree he flies off course, he will miss his target by 92 feet for every mile flown.
- For every 60 miles he flies, he will miss his target by one mile.
- Flying around the equator will land him almost 500 miles off target.[4]

Stick to your game plan. Stay on course. Don't stray even a degree no matter what distractions may try to steer you in a different direction. Remain on the course so you can land in your specified destination.

Reflection Questions:

1. Can you work your game plan on your own, or do you need an outside perspective to help you?
2. What is your initial "why"? (this could change)
3. What is one little thing you could change now to begin the baby steps toward your goal?
4. Can you tell when things are trying to take you off course, even just a degree?
5. Is there anything in your life trying to take you off course currently?
6. What is your tolerance level for being off course?

Further Reading:

-   Psalm 37:4-6
-   Proverbs 16:9

Application: Create a game plan

-   Download the "Questions for Your Game Plan" PDF
-   Download the "Questions for Your Race Plan" PDF
-   Complete the "Think It Through" worksheet

Note: You can find the "Think It Through" worksheet and the "Questions for Your Gameplan" and "Questions for Your Race Plan" PDFs at www.redhotmindset.com/MOMresources

Chapter 6

Trust Your Race Plan

*"Trust in the Lord with all your heart and lean not
on your own understanding; in all your ways acknowledge Him,
and He will make your paths straight."*
– Proverbs 3:5-6

Wrestlers all have their favorite starting position, whether it's up, down, or neutral. In between periods, they look to their coach to find out which position they should choose for the start of next period. There are times when the coach will direct them into their least favorite position on purpose because they have insight into the situational advantage. It's up to the wrestler to be willing to drop his ego and trust his coach, knowing his coach has a clear vision of the mat, has sights on the opponent, and knows how the current score comes into play. Maybe the coach wants the wrestler to develop in a weaker position now, so he can wrestle with greater confidence in much more meaningful matches later in the season. The coach has a long-term vision in the athlete's success.

Just as the wrestler needs to trust his coach, we need faith in three areas as we press on toward our dreams: Faith in our plan, faith in our coach, and faith in ourselves. Because even with the perfect plan, or perfect coach, it all comes down to our own ability to work through obstacles, create disciplined habits, and minimize distractions.

BELIEVE IT WILL WORK FOR YOU

For my fourth marathon, I needed to trust the game plan. I realized I never really had a solid game plan before. In the past, I had hodge-podged together a race training that I thought would work. This time I decided I needed a specific plan that I knew had results. My husband's aunt introduced me to an unfamiliar training method. She was training for Grandma's Marathon right alongside me, so having that support was key.

I looked at the training plan and noticed that it was a run/walk method and assumed that it wouldn't work for me. How could walking help me to shave sixteen minutes off my best marathon time? It seemed rather impossible or even foolish.

Looking into the run/walk method further, I discovered some key insights that proponents point out about the plan. The main purpose is to reduce stress on both the body and mind. It allows the running muscles a short break and also gives runners a mental break.

The idea behind the strategy is that the continuous use of the running muscles will result in quicker fatigue. By adding in short fifteen to sixty second walk breaks, runners tap into different muscles, and the running muscles recover easier. It creates a form of interval training and also helps to keep body temperature lower. It can help regulate a runner's heart rate so it doesn't peak and remain high throughout the entire race. And, obviously, it helps runners to conserve the energy and resources they will need to get them to the finish line.

Ultimately, I trust my husband's aunt, so I decided to move forward with the training plan. I never expected how drastically it would increase my speed in such a short timeframe. Because it essentially becomes an interval workout, the run portion is quicker than the desired race pace, but the walks help balance things with a short recovery. It is supposed to be able to help runners keep the pace consistent as well as cut finish times.

In my half marathon and 15k races that spring, I used the run/walk method as practice runs, and it quickly made me a believer in this newfound method. I was skeptical up to the day of the half marathon, but after seeing the results, I am a convert. In that half marathon, I finished ninth out of nine hundred and sixty-six runners. This was new territory for me. I had never placed in a race, nor had I ever truly had that as a goal or forethought.

The game plan is everything. Whatever game plan you have, you need to trust it. You need to be a believer in what you are doing. Not just believing that it will work, but believing that it will work for you.

GOALS TAKE TIME

Goals take time. Just because you set a goal, doesn't mean it's going to happen overnight. They take time to develop, and they take time to achieve. Goals help us to be future focused and keep our eyes on the vision. To see it through, we need to have long-term thought process rather than an instant-gratification mentality.

Leave The Past In The Past

Nothing can change until you change your mind. Your thinking needs to change first. How you see yourself needs to change. You need to look to the future and forget about the past. The Israelites wandered the wilderness for forty years for this very reason. They began looking back at their past as Egyptian slaves, put on rose-colored glasses, and figured it wasn't so bad. After all, they had "provision" while there. They began justifying the brutal life they had survived in Egypt, forgetting how miserable their years of slavery were.

It's like the character Brooks in *The Shawshank Redemption*; he longed for his jail cell again because it was easier to let someone else care for him. It sounds ridiculous. Who wouldn't want to be free? But the Israelites longed for their jail cell back. Their minds tricked them to recall the past as more pleasurable than it was rather than to take responsibility for their future and step into God's call and promises for their lives.

Leave your past in the past, don't look back at it. Don't let your mind wander to the "good ole days." The past can't change, but you can change your future. The late Myles Monroe, author of *Burden of Freedom*, stated it perfectly when he said, "God will never allow you to become all you were born to be until you are sick of being what you were."

Stick With It When It Gets Hard

When the going gets tough, the tough get going. Cliché, I know, but so true. Trials will come. Circumstances won't always be in your favor, but nothing exceptional happens without a fight. Are you willing to stick it out? Are you willing to go through the fire if need be? Trusting the game plan means you're willing to practice intensely, whether you want to or not. To be honest, you're never going to really feel like doing anything. Naturally, we like the easy route, so we need to separate our feelings from our action.

Feelings can change quickly. Take the frazzled mom who is angry at her kids for fighting and bouncing all over the house. She's raising her voice, threatening punishments, and completely frustrated. Her facial expressions tell it all. Then, the phone rings. She's still angry and mumbling frustrations all the way to the phone, but, paradoxically, she answers the call with, "Hello!" in the sweetest voice possible. All of the sudden, she's laughing and smiling about whatever the person on the other end of the receiver is saying and all those angry feelings disappear as if nothing ever happened. You've seen it! I know you have. I just might even be guilty of it myself!

Feelings are a bit bipolar. They come and go quickly and fiercely. We would never finish anything if we relied on our feelings. Your flesh wants to take the easy route. It wants to come home from a long day at work and relax on the couch in front of the television with a large bowl of ice cream. Your flesh doesn't want to have to put in more effort than it has to. If it feels hard, it doesn't want to do it. You need to find a way to bottle up these feelings and stay the course.

When it's hard, you need to be willing to keep going. Hard equals testing grounds. The Israelites were stranded in the desert for FORTY YEARS when it should have only taken them forty days to walk from Egypt to Canaan. They missed out on a land filled with milk and honey and all the good things that God wanted for them simply because they chose to whine and complain and failed the test. Because the Israelites kept failing their test, God proceeded to make them take it, again and again. The first generation never even got to smell the Promised Land because they couldn't figure it out. They weren't willing to stick with it when it was hard. They weren't willing to listen to their coach. They weren't willing to believe that they could defeat the Canaanites. The root of the problem was that they didn't believe in themselves.

Get to the hard and push through. Pass the test so you can move on. Don't get stuck in the desert for forty years when your Promised Land may only be forty days away.

Don't Look At Results Right Away

Goals and dreams take time. Writing a book has been a dream of mine for years. Even this book has been on my heart and mind for more than five years. However, I know that goals take time. I finished this book a full year before it launched, which felt like an excruciating amount of time to wait, but I didn't want to rush it. We can't rush our goals because things need to align and come together.

I knew I needed that year to set myself up for success. I needed that year to form launch strategies so that my book would get noticed. I wanted to take my dream and inspire others and actually be effective in the process. I didn't want to write a book just to write a book. I didn't want to create something that would just sit on the shelf and collect dust. I wanted to write a book that could be effective and help others to see their potential and be inspired to pursue it. I wanted to create a longing in others to dream again and to follow those dreams to fruition.

It took about five years to come together, and the last year and a half was when I did the majority of the work. But all those years, even the dreaming that I did, created a pull for me to finish. For a period of time, it was just a dream. I hadn't made a definite decision yet and was just dreaming it up in my head, imagining all the possibilities. It took time. It took time for me to believe in me. It took time to build up the confidence that said, yes, I can do it. The time is now.

Just remember, goals and dreams take time. Don't look for results right away because they won't be there. Patience means you are willing to take the action consistently and wait it out. The results won't come without the action, but it's the everyday habits you create that bring the results. Over time.

Don't Compare

Comparison is the number one killer of success. In the times of social media, we see everyone's best day, best hair, and best relationships. The problem is that we tend to compare our worst to someone else's best. We only see the positive on the computer screen—the cute and well-behaved kids, the perfect family pictures, the job promotions. We don't see everyday life, yet we seem to compare our lives to that fairytale picture of what we think others have.

Comparison will steal your joy. When you start comparing your life to others', you begin to feel less contentment in your own. You may start having a woe-is-me attitude and begin questioning why you can't have what they have. Why do the job promotions always seem to pass you up? Why does it seem like they have so much time to spend with friends when it seems like all you have time for is work? How can they always keep their house so clean? How did they get that nice car or home? How do they have such well-behaved kids, and it seems like yours are fighting all the time? Why do they get all the breaks?

Comparison can lead to resentment of others and can create a barrier to your own success. The interesting thing is, when you are so busy comparing yourself to others, you automatically pass by all the opportunities around you. Comparison will blind you to your own growth and opportunities. It will distract you from seeking your own success.

In all honesty, life isn't always fair. We may go through harder times than a friend or family member and wonder why they get it so easy and wish that for ourselves. But what we have to remember is that they only show their highlight reels. We don't really know the exact details of what is going on behind the scenes.

Everyone has his own struggles. Maybe they already had a season of hard that they had to plow through to get to the other side. We don't know. Some of us go through more than others. I have no idea why. But I do know that God will never give us more than we can handle. I know that He will be with us every step of the way if we let Him, and that is a true advantage.

Have faith in your own plan and your own timeline. Life may not seem fair, but if we press through, we can have victory. Comparison can hinder your drive and passion. It can stop you in your tracks. It will take you off your focus. Don't waste the precious time you have by comparing yourself to others!

Opinions Of Others

People may try to talk you out of the vision that God has put in your heart. You need to make sure that you are focused on what you know you are called to do, and don't let people talk you out of it. Don't let them convince you that you're not worthy or that it's not going to happen. They don't really know the journey you are embarking on. They don't know because they lack vision.

You cannot be a people pleaser and accomplish your dream. You can't please all people all the time, and that's a fact. Someone isn't going to approve of what you're doing or even of who you are. Are you really going to let that stop you from doing what God has called you to do? People pleasers end up burning out because they do all, and are all to all people, and lack the time to fill themselves back up. Unfortunately, they lose out on pursuing the true passions of their heart.

Others' disbelief in you and your dreams usually has nothing to do with you at all. It really comes from an insecurity deep within themselves. It's almost a coping mechanism for them to talk bad about you so they don't have to feel so bad about themselves and their lack of ambition. Don't let others, no matter who it is, talk you out of your dream.

CONTROL THE CONTROLLABLES

No matter how good your plan is, things will happen to you along the way that are completely outside of your control. You need to practice the art of recognizing what is and isn't in your control and let go of what is not. It's not worth holding onto something we have no control over. We can, however, get our plan back on track by taking responsibility for the things we can control—and we need to. We need to learn how to control the controllables.

What's Not Controllable?

To be honest, there are probably more things that aren't controllable than are controllable. We need to be okay with the fact that many things are out of our control, and we need to pre-plan how we are going to think about these things and what we are going to do when issues arise.

What we CAN'T control in RUNNING:

- The weather
- How we feel on race day
- The race course
- Injury
- Other racers

What we CAN'T control in LIFE:

- The unknown
- Other people (their opinion of you, how they think, how they feel, what they do, how they react)
- Change
- Circumstances
- The past
- Where we came from

Isn't it funny that we can recognize when other people are focused on the uncontrollables, but it's hard to see when we do the exact same thing in the midst of our own struggles? Focusing on the uncontrollables can be paralyzing and keep us from moving forward.

When there are uncontrollables in our lives, and it seems like we cannot help but ruminate in them, we need to find a way to distract ourselves. When we do this, our minds can no longer continually play back the things out of our control, and we can focus in on what is controllable.

This distraction of the mind may look different for everyone, but when you begin to ruminate on the uncontrollables in your life, find a task to work on, pray, read a book, or choose a mantra to repeat. Do this every time the uncontrollables try to grab hold of your emotions and peace. A positive distraction will keep you on the right track, and eventually it will become easier to focus in on the controllables and away from circumstances out of your control.

What Is Controllable?

There are only two things that you have complete control over—your actions and your attitudes. How do you choose to see adversity? Successful people with a winning attitude find the best in every situation and do not allow for circumstances to define them. Rather, they let the circumstances refine them.

Two things we CAN control:

1. Our Actions: How we prepare, our discipline, our training, our rest and nutrition, how we speak, who we associate with, what we read or hear, who we listen to.

2. Our Attitude: our emotions, our effort, our focus, our positive mentality, our coachability, our perspective, our thoughts, our beliefs, our gratitude.

We need to work on what we can control—our actions and our attitude—and we need to leave the rest to God. How we react to a situation is in our control. How we discipline ourselves is in our control. How we feel is in our control. How we think is in our control.

We may not be able to control where we came from, but we can definitely influence where we're headed through our own personal growth and change. Proverbs 16:9 says, "In their hearts humans plan their course,

91

but the Lord establishes their steps." Even though God holds the reins, we need to proactively influence our path and personal growth. We can't control our past, and we can't control natural events, but we can influence the direction of our future. We can't control how other people feel about us, what they do, how they react, but we can control our fear of what others think.

We need to choose to focus on the things within our control. Focusing on the uncontrollables only causes worry and stress and all things negative. It can cause us to slow down or stop altogether because things look or seem impossible. How freeing it is when you know that all the things that you're choosing to focus on are within your control!

MINIMIZE DISTRACTIONS

Distractions come in all forms and are things that inhibit us from keeping our eyes on the goal. A distraction is "a thing that prevents someone from giving full attention to something else."[1] It's a disturbance, interference, or an interruption. Distractions can be small or large. Distractions can easily take you off your game and hinder you from moving forward. They can distract you from your plan, slow your progress, and cause you to doubt your dream.

Cell Phones

Cell phones are a common, and often overlooked, source of distraction. According to a study done by Global Tech Protection and support company Asurion, on average, Americans check their cell phones once every twelve minutes, which equates to eighty times a day![2] American adults spend on average two hours and fifty-one minutes on their smartphones every day, according to comScore's 2017 report.[3] These statistics are shocking, yet completely believable. Here are some tips to minimize cell phone distractions:

1. Silence your phone while being productive. When you're in the mode, put your phone out of arm's reach.

2. Turn off notifications so it doesn't alert you every time you get a call, text, tweet, email, etc.

3. Go into the settings on your phone and physically see how much time you are spending on specific apps. It's fairly enlightening. It will alert you to how distractible you really are.

4. Leave your phone in a different room for a period of time. I promise you, if someone has an emergency, they will figure out a way to get a hold of you.

Television

On average, adults in the U.S. watch five hours of television per day, according to a Nielsen report.[4] That's around seventy-seven days per year! Just think of where you could be if you were to cut even just one hour a day from watching TV and put that time toward accomplishing your goals. Here are some ways to discipline your TV watching habit:

1. Cut the cable. Consider eliminating the distraction altogether by cutting back on the number of channels you have readily available. You may also save upwards of $200-$300 a month!

2. Unsubscribe from Netflix or Hulu. Ask yourself the question, "Does watching shows get me closer to my goal?" These platforms are cheaper alternatives to cable, but they can also be more addicting. I know. I used to be caught up in many marathon binges of watching shows, not even because they were good, but just because each episode leaves you hanging and wanting to know what happens next.

3. Choose a limit for yourself. Watching TV isn't bad. It can even be fun! Choose a limit of how much you will allow yourself to watch so it doesn't become a distraction or addiction. Is it one show a day? Is it one hour a day? Find a balance that you can stick to.

4. Use television as a reward. Finish what you set out to do for the day and reward yourself with a show before bedtime.

Email

Checking email can lull you into a false sense of productivity, so limit checking it. Sometimes the need to be doing something makes me check my email more than I should. Consider checking your email one to two times a day. Maybe plan a specific time to do so, after breakfast or before dinner for example. It is plenty okay to make someone wait twenty-four hours for a response.

If you can, don't take your work home with you. Home time should equal home time. Consider removing your work email from your phone entirely. If you need to answer work emails off the clock, plan specific times throughout the day to check it. Don't be a slave to it. If you answer your emails immediately, in the long run, you will be expected to continue that habit.

Keep A To-Do List

Prioritize your day by writing down everything that needs to get done. Star the items that are most important or timely, and begin there. Choose what you need to get done that day, and go to work. A list will help you stay focused and on track.

Overscheduling

Get good at saying no. At least for a time, it may be valuable to limit the activities that you participate in. If you are always saying yes, then people are going to expect you to bend over backward for them. It is good to help others, but you need to know your limits and your margins. If you say "No" first, you can always come back to them and say "Yes." Doing the opposite is much harder and more offensive. Make "No" your first answer.

Clutter

Physical clutter can actually harm your creative juices. Clutter can stress you out and create a less peaceful work environment. I have made it a habit to take twenty minutes a day to continually declutter and create a peaceful space. I work to keep my kitchen and living room clutter free since those are the rooms we live in the most. With kids in the house, it is bound to get messy, but just twenty minutes a day can make a huge impact. I know this feels like a continual struggle, but here are a few tips to make this happen:

1. Make it a habit to declutter or clean 20-30 minutes a day. Listen to a success podcast while you work!

2. Involve your kids. Choose a chore a day for the kids to help with. This will create a sense of responsibility for them but also not overwhelm them. It's amazing what many hands can do in a short period of time.

3. Limit what you bring into the house. Choose contentment over quantity. The more items in the house, the more clutter you will feel. Fewer toys means kids need to use their imaginations more. Fewer clothes means less laundry to fold. Less kitchenware means less dishes. Choose to live with less.

These tips may seem unrelated to your dream. However, eliminating distractions will allow you to focus on your plan and devote more time to accomplishing it.

FAITH VS. FEAR

"Now faith is confidence in what we hope for and assurance about what we do not see." (Hebrews 11:1) In essence, faith is complete trust in something or someone, whether there is physical evidence present or not. It's the confidence in a planned result. Fear, on the other hand, is unbelief. Fear could also be defined as faith that something bad may happen. It plays on our emotions and can stop us from pressing on toward our goal.

Faith And Fear Cannot Coexist

Faith equals trust. If I don't trust, I'm really just faithless. Don't allow fear to creep in and steal your belief. Fear and faith are oppositions. There is a Godly fear, also known as reverence, that may be present with faith, but for the most part, faith and fear cannot coexist.

When Noah was told to build an ark, even though he had never experienced rain a day in his life, he actually had a mix of fear and faith. "By FAITH Noah, when warned about things not yet seen, in holy FEAR built an ark to save his family. By his faith he condemned the world and became heir of the righteousness that is in keeping with the faith" (Hebrews 11:7).

The difference in this is that it was a godly fear that he had. He believed that what God said was true. He believed this "flood" would destroy the earth just as God said it would, even though he had no idea what a flood was. He had a righteous, healthy fear, and because of that, he was willing to trust the ultimate plan and build the ark.

When I talk about faith and fear not being able to coexist, I'm talking about an unhealthy fear of something that may or may not ever happen. You know those people I'm talking about who are always worried about catching a disease, getting into a car accident, someone breaking into their house, and the list goes on. You can't be in true expectation when fear is present. Fear causes apprehension. Fear causes anxiety. In contrast, faith says no matter what is thrown my way, no matter my circumstances, I will push through and trust in the end goal. Faith says I will trust in God, I will trust in my coach, I will trust in my calling, and I will persevere.

In the same way that we talked about finding a distraction over the uncontrollables, we can do this when fear arises. When fear tries to steal our faith or our peace, we need to have a positive mantra ready to speak over it, such as "Fear has no control over me," or "I choose to trust my game plan and push past the fear." Find a song that resonates with you about overcoming, and play it when fear creeps up. Remind yourself that you are worthy, and you are strong, and you will not let fear play a part in what you are doing. Read a positive book that will keep your mentality and emotions in check. These are a few activities you can do to keep the faith and ward off fear.

Don't Worry

Worry contradicts trust and faith. Nothing good comes from worry. We can work ourselves up over things that will probably never happen. This reminds me of the story about a woman who was overcome with fear. At night this woman was extremely worried about the possibility of a burglar breaking into their house.

The worry kept her awake, and every little noise stiffened her spine. Her husband couldn't stand how much control this fear had over her life—not to mention all he wanted was a good night's sleep without having to check the locks on every window and door beforehand!

This worry continued for years until one night there was a sudden noise downstairs. Fearfully, this woman made her husband go downstairs to see what the commotion was. Her prophecy became self-fulfilled, as he came face to face with an actual burglar! Surprisingly, he felt more relief than fear and welcomed the stranger saying, "Finally! I need you to come upstairs and meet my wife! She has been waiting for you for years!"

The word tells us that just as God clothes the fields and feeds the birds, so will he take care of us. "Therefore, do not worry about tomorrow, for tomorrow will worry about itself." (Matthew 6:34)

How To Handle Doubt

No matter how much faith you have, doubt and fear will continually try to creep in, but you have to learn how to shut them down immediately. An effective way to do that is to speak to the doubt. We will talk more in depth about this in a later chapter, but the only way to stop a negative thought is through a positive word.

When doubt comes, go to your coach or mentor. Be honest about how you are feeling. A mentor can't give you direction if he doesn't know exactly what you are dealing with. There needs to be a mutual trust that it is a safe place for you to share your struggles and desires.

It's important to have a sounding board and someone who can speak life to you in those vulnerable moments. A mentor can be that person without having the emotional attachment to you. Family members and friends will lean more to the side of feeling sorry for you. A mentor will challenge you to keep moving forward.

The summer before I had our third child, I felt in my spirit that I would leave my full-time work the following year. It wasn't until I felt that conviction, and decided to trust and pursue it, that I found out I was pregnant with our third child. The next spring turned out to be the perfect time for me to leave my job—or so we thought. However, the day I left on maternity leave was the day my husband also came home—his job had let him go because of "restructuring." Talk about a faith stretcher!

What were we going to do? We had just made the decision that I was supposed to be home, we both felt that it was something God had called us to, but now this giant problem stared us down. Doubt crept in. It was hard to keep those negative thoughts and fears from rising up and taking over. In the back of my mind, I knew that I could still go back to work if I needed to. I hadn't given my notice because I was still on maternity leave. There was a safeguard in that, though my spirit said, "No, don't give in." It became an obedience factor. Would I succumb to the fears and go back to work, or would I take that leap of faith and trust that God had a plan? If I am not obedient, then I am automatically in disobedience. That's a tough pill to swallow.

The end of my maternity leave was quickly approaching, and it was decision time. I remember writing my letter of resignation and sitting down to coffee with my boss. The knot in my stomach was real, but I knew that I was in obedience. My boss had so much respect for my decision and even said he wished he had that kind of faith. The cool story that came out of this is that he actually took that same leap of faith a few months later! He answered the call to do something for himself, and I believe it stemmed from me standing my ground in faith.

Months passed, and my husband still hadn't found a job. It was about seven months before a new opportunity finally came. Here's the positive to that story. It was a better job, better pay, and a better opportunity for our family. We never fell behind, and our needs were taken care of the entire time we were both jobless. We lived on less, but we never felt like we suffered.

There's so much more to that story, but the main point of it is that we just trusted in the process. We trusted what we believed was God's plan. We overcame doubt every day. Doubt never permanently goes away. It is a daily battle we have to fight. We just choose to live in faith and not let fear overtake us.

HELP! I GOT OFF TRACK!

Life happens. No matter how disciplined or passionate we are, there will be times when we get pulled off track. Maybe we took our eyes off the end goal, or maybe we got stuck in the process rather than the purpose, or maybe it's due to an unpleasant circumstance, or maybe we looked back and let our past define us, or maybe we allowed distractions to take our attention. No matter the reason, realizing you're off track and taking steps to get back on course is all you really need to do. There are four steps necessary to be successful launching forward once again: re-calibrate with your coach, forgive yourself, start where you're at, and restart with experience.

Recalibrate With Your Coach

Don't dodge your coach or mentor. It's natural to want to hide when things aren't going right because we want to be displayed in the best light possible to them. Adam and Eve hid from God after eating the forbidden fruit and realizing they had disobeyed his command.

When we open up to our mentor, our ego is on the line. But, when it comes to having a mentor, we need to be willing to drop our egos and have an open, honest relationship. We need to be willing to share the good, the bad, and the ugly with them. If we don't, they can't help us continue to grow.

If you're in a mentorship relationship, you need to be able to take constructive criticism without taking offense. A mentor isn't in your life to make you feel good and keep things all hunky dory. A mentor will help expose your weaknesses in order to help you change your mindset. A mentor will help you see things in a different light. A mentor wants to see you succeed, but sometimes hard conversations need to take place in order

99

for that to happen. Offense is your choice. You choose how to interpret what someone says, which means you choose whether to take offense or not. A genuine mentor has your best intentions in mind.

If you get off track and have a coach, one of the best ways to figure things out is to connect with him. Coaches have most likely gone through similar struggles, which is why they are where they are. Drop your ego at the door, choose not to take offense, and ask your coach to pour wisdom into your life.

Forgive Yourself

Don't beat yourself up. You are harder on yourself than on anyone else. Remember, you are your toughest critic. It's easier to help others through their problems. We happily dish out advice and don't think twice. We encourage our friends to pick themselves up. We tell them to go easy on themselves. We tell them not to give themselves a hard time when things don't go their way. We tell them to forgive themselves. We tell them mistakes happen, but it's totally normal, and those mistakes can transform into learning experiences for them.

It's time we take our own advice and give ourselves a break. We are not perfect, nor will we ever be. We will make mistake after mistake, and we need to respect ourselves enough to forgive ourselves and move on. It takes time to learn a new skill, develop a new habit, or reach a goal. It's not about perfection, it's about excellence. Strive toward becoming an excellent person in all that you do but recognize you will never be perfect. Recognize when you are being your worst critic and shut that down immediately.

Start Where You're At

Don't wait for circumstances to be perfect. They never will be. You're not even capable of learning without being in motion. Remember, trusting the game plan means that you're willing to practice intensely. You're never going to feel like doing something, but your coach can't even help you unless you're in the midst of your battle. You can't steer a parked car.

You need to be in the heat to light on fire. My mentor ingrained in me that we don't feel our way into acting; we act our way into feeling.

Wherever you are, there you are. Don't wait for the right time. That time will never come. Don't wait until you get approval from others. Some will never give it. Don't wait until your kids are older. They're watching you now. Don't wait until you feel ready. You never will be. Make the decision to start where you're at. No matter where that is. Just start.

Restart With Experience

Let's admit it, no one likes to lose. Most of the time, failure is frowned upon, but failure is actually necessary to success. Think of failure as learning grounds. Without it, there's really nothing to learn and no adversity to overcome. There is no victory without adversity. Getting off track is normal, but many choose to stay there.

When you get off track or "fail," take that and grow with it. Now you have experience under your belt and a greater perspective to go off of when you start again. Don't let failure take you out. Do as leadership author and coach John Maxwell says, and "fail forward." Let that failure drive you to try again differently. Let it teach you something. Let it move you on. Get excited about failure because it means you're one step closer to winning—if you choose to restart with experience.

FINAL STRETCH

Remember talking about chess in the prior chapter? The best strategy in chess is to focus on the end game. Don't become overwhelmed by the many moves or ways things could go. Simply continue to trod on and look toward the future. Don't remain in the past. Press forward and stick with your game plan. Trust the game plan. Trust your coach. Trust yourself.

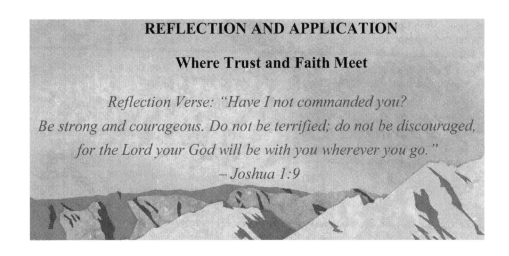

REFLECTION AND APPLICATION

Where Trust and Faith Meet

Reflection Verse: "Have I not commanded you?
Be strong and courageous. Do not be terrified; do not be discouraged,
for the Lord your God will be with you wherever you go."
– Joshua 1:9

One of the most difficult things to do is to truly trust. It takes vulnerability and openness. It takes letting down our guard and risking our egos. God says to trust Him in everything. He cares about every minor detail of our lives, and He wants to lead us, but he cannot without our will. Trust and faith coexist. You cannot have faith without trusting God's promises. Trusting God's game plan may mean changing our plan to fit His. True trust means we will implement what our coach directs us to do, even if we don't understand the purpose right away. True trust means letting go of doubt and pressing on in faith. Allow God to use you to see His plans through. In His will is the most precious place to be.

Reflection Questions:

1. What would you need to let go of in order to have a mentor speak into your life? (i.e. control, guard, ego, etc)

2. Why is it hard to let your guard down and trust your mentor?

3. What worries do you need to let go of?

4. Does your problem handle you, or do you handle your problem?

Further Reading:

- Matthew 6:25-34
- Isaiah 41:10
- Proverbs 11:14
- Proverbs 15:22

Application: Find a coach/mentor who can speak into your life.

1. Make sure the person has what you want.
2. Make sure the person is personally growing.
3. Make sure the person is willing to speak truth into your life. It's important that this person isn't just a cheerleader, but rather someone who's not willing to see you stay where you are.

Chapter 7

Get Tough

"Desire is the key to motivation, but it's determination and commitment to an unrelenting pursuit of your goal—a commitment to excellence—that will enable you to attain the success you seek."
– Mario Andretti

After a terrible accident in 1917, eight-year-old Glenn Cunningham was told he would be a cripple for the rest of his life. He and his older brother had one job to tend to before school—to fill the coal stove with kerosene so the quaint Kansas schoolhouse would be warmed for class.

One morning, someone mistakenly filled the kerosene container with gasoline. As soon as they lit the stove, it caused a massive explosion. Not only did Glenn lose his thirteen-year-old brother in the schoolhouse fire, but he also was in rough shape. Left more dead than alive, his legs were badly burned.

Doctors recommended amputation of his legs and predicted he would never walk again. They said he definitely had no chance. He lost all the flesh on his knees and shins and all the toes on his left foot. The doctors even went as far as to tell his parents that it may have been better for him to have died in the explosion rather than be crippled for a lifetime. His parents refused amputation.

Glenn, however, understood determination at a very young age. He not only spoke that he would walk again, but he said he would run. It took much desire and fight, but he began the painful process of learning to stand, and he eventually did regain the ability to walk. What he discovered was that "it hurt like thunder to walk, but it didn't hurt at all when I ran, so for five or six years, about all I did was run."

He not only defied the odds and learned to walk again, he became a runner—and not just an ordinary runner. He became an American distance runner who was considered by many to be the greatest American miler of all time. He was nicknamed the "Kansas Flyer." He went on to compete in two summer Olympics and took fourth in 1932 and silver in 1936 in the 1500-meter race. In 1934 he set the world record mile run at 4:06.8.[1]

He clung to Isaiah 40:31, "But those who hope in the Lord will renew their strength. They will soar on wings like eagles; they will run and not grow weary, they will walk and not be faint."

So what was the difference maker for Glenn Cunningham? He wasn't any different than you and me. What he had was a burning desire to walk again and a relentless determination to prove those doctors wrong. He chose to become mentally tough.

CHOOSE DISCIPLINE

Pain or circumstances can paralyze us from pressing on, but successful people are disciplined people. They have learned not to give into their fleshly desires, but rather to do the things they need to do to drive them to where they want to go. They have learned that the key is in their daily routine.

John Maxwell, renowned author and leadership coach, has said if he were to come to your house for a day and spend time with you, with about a 95 percent accuracy, he would be able to tell you how successful you are and how successful you are going to be. How can he do this? Well, if he spends ten hours with you, he will be able to effectively see what your daily routine is, and he says, "The secret of your success is discovered in your daily agenda."[2] He says our success is based on the daily decisions we make and the daily disciplines we practice. I completely agree. What we do daily determines our greater outcome.

Throughout this chapter, we are going to talk through three different kinds of discipline that are important to achieving your goals: physical, mental, and emotional.

Making It Personal

When I was training for my third marathon (my second attempt to qualify for Boston), I was working full time at my regular job with irregular hours, overnight at a fitness facility, coordinating a mom's group, and homeschooling my oldest boy. I would say I could have used every excuse to quit, and no one would have questioned me. In all actuality, they probably would have praised me for it.

I ran on a few hours of sleep most nights and hardly saw my family, but somehow I was able to uphold all the responsibilities I had. Though we didn't have hours of quality time, my family never thought I was neglecting them. I never gave up my training in the process, it just looked different. It was a choice for me to train. I worked out at 5 a.m. after my overnight shifts and before I went to sleep for a few hours.

Many called me crazy and told me I was burning the candle at both ends. Looking back, I have no idea how I got through that season, and I did want to quit multiple times. Fortunately, I had developed a strong dream and was willing to make sacrifices to see it through. I did not become disciplined overnight, but I worked hard to establish habits that would lead me closer to my dream.

Discipline Defined

A disciplined person has trained himself to do something in a controlled way, creating habits in his daily routine. Discipline provides the physical, mental or emotional training necessary to accomplish the desired goal. Self-discipline is not an innate characteristic. It is a learned skill and can be developed in anyone who chooses to hone it.

Willpower is a moment by moment choice. Many say, "I don't have the willpower to pass up that piece of chocolate cake," or, "I don't have the will power to get up an hour earlier to get a workout in." Everyone has desires toward something—losing weight, gaining muscle, advancing at work, starting a business. Here's the thing. When they say, "I don't have the willpower to…" what they are really saying is, "I choose not to do…" Saying "I don't have the willpower" is an excuse to be lazy or to justify staying stagnant and not moving forward. Anybody can develop the willpower if he so chooses to.

The only way to increase your discipline is to intentionally practice it in your daily routine. It's easy to come up with a list of habits that you want to do every day, and it's even easy enough to figure out how to fit them into your day, but what is difficult is being intentional when practicing each habit each day.

If you're not intentional, you'll just go through the motions and get stuck in a rut. Intentional means you select the habits and disciplines necessary to attaining your goal, but you also determine the purpose or why behind each habit. Then when you are practicing the desired habits, you are also doing them with the intention to grow and change and move closer to your finish line.

The definition of insanity is doing the same thing over and over again and expecting a different result. This is no different. Habits are meant to help you get and stay on track. Once you're on track, then keep going. Continue to assess how your habits are helping you. Do you need to adjust anything? Do you need to add or subtract any habits? Do you need to re-evaluate a habit and increase it? Is what you're doing today getting you closer to your goals for tomorrow?

The late Myles Munroe, leadership consultant and minister, said, "Without mental transformation, the actions we take to 'change' may only produce a new place where we continue to do our old things." Don't have a checklist mentality. Know why you're doing what you're doing and the result you intend each action to have. Find purpose in your daily disciplines.

Follow Through With Action No Matter What

Two words: resilience and determination. These are what you need to develop in order to become a disciplined person. Resilience means "the capacity to recover quickly from difficulties; toughness. The ability of a substance or object to spring back into shape; elasticity."[3] Determination means "firmness of purpose; resolute."[4]

Resilience, essentially, means to be tough. We all know difficulties will come our way. We are going to have failure in our lives. How quickly will we regain focus and get back after it? A resilient person knows he will fail but is also willing to get up every time he gets pushed down. A resilient person adapts well in the face of adversity, trauma, or other stresses.

Nylon is a resilient substance. No matter how much it is stretched, pulled, or prodded, it always seems to find the shape it was designed to have. That's resilience. You will be stretched out of your comfort zone. You will be pulled in different directions. You will be prodded by those who don't understand. Will you be able to be resilient and bounce back? Don't let adversity define you. Be resilient.

A determined person is firm in his purpose. He is resolved to do what he needs to do no matter what trials or tribulations may get in his way. Everyone experiences bad training days. The day was just off. The weather was out of control, windy, and cold. Last night's sleep was miserable. Bad days happen. Determination means resolving to stick with the plan in lieu of what the day brings. Don't let the day define what you do.

Be determined to pursue your dreams. Do the steps until you get it. Don't let the training or action required beat you. Do it until you get it right. Keep doing it until you can't get it wrong. When you get to the point where your habits and disciplines are non-negotiables no matter what life throws at you, you know you are now a determined person.

You can trust your game plan all you want. You can have a definite belief in it. You can visualize it and study it with vigor. That alone, though, will not get you to your dream. You can trust in the game plan, but at the end of the day, you still need to do something for it to work for you. Without action, your game plan becomes null.

PHYSICAL DISCIPLINE

Successful people do what others are unwilling to do. Successful people watch the masses and do the opposite. When the masses are watching television, successful people are reading. When the masses are listening to music on the radio, successful people are listening to mindset podcasts. Successful people choose to focus. They choose to get physically tough.

Beat Your Body To Make It Your Slave

Discipline equals doing the things you don't want to do. Motivational speaker Terri Savelle Foy says that how you do one thing is how you'll do everything. That statement is so true and so incredibly powerful! It's hard to be disciplined in one area and not in all the others. In the same way, if you're not disciplined in one area, most likely you just aren't a disciplined person.

The problem is, discipline isn't easy. It isn't easy, but it is a choice. It's a daily choice. It's a moment by moment choice. Disciplined people have learned how to overcome their feelings and do what they need to no matter what.

A mantra that I had been playing over and over in my mind during my hard season of training was, "I beat my body to make it my slave." (1 Corinthians 9:27) I still reflect on this statement and use it as one of my daily affirmations. Now, I don't physically beat myself, but I do put my flesh under submission. What this means is that I make my body, or my flesh, do what I tell it to do. I don't let my body or my feelings dictate what I do. I do what I know to be right and what I know will move me forward—whether I like it or not.

Let's look at a few other translations of 1 Corinthians 9:27:

- "I discipline my body like an athlete, training it to do what it should do." (NLT)
- "I discipline my body and bring it under strict control." (CBS)
- "I keep on disciplining my body, making it serve me." (ISV)

- "I batter my body and bring it into servitude." (BLB)

Do you see a pattern? Each version talks about how discipline is putting your flesh under your control so your body does what you tell it to do whether it wants to or not. A disciplined person doesn't make excuses. A disciplined person gets the job done. Choose to become a disciplined person.

Habits are regular practices we create for a given purpose. Once created, habits are hard to give up. This is good news... but it's also bad news. A habit that moves you forward and grows you as a person is a good habit, one you want to create. But, unfortunately, it's easier to create bad habits without even knowing it. It seems bad habits are slightly addicting.

When you get home from work, what is your daily ritual? Do you tend to sit down on the couch, turn on the television, and find yourself engrossed in your favorite shows? When you go to bed, do you bring your phone with you and tend to mindlessly scroll social media only to realize two hours later that you should have gone to sleep? Do you have a habit of hitting snooze five times before you finally get up and realize you only have fifteen minutes to get ready, eat, and get out the door? On your way to work, do you have a habit of cranking up the music and jamming out? All these things seem harmless, but done enough, they create habits, recurrent rituals, and they drag you away from success.

Just think if you were to change one little thing. The average American spends more than eleven hours a day interacting with media, whether listening to, watching, or reading.[5] Can you take one of those hours and put it toward your dream? Maybe instead of coming home and sitting on the couch right away after work, you take thirty minutes to sit down and write. Maybe instead of bringing your phone to bed with you, you leave it out in the living room so you go to sleep when you intended. Maybe you choose to hit snooze once instead of multiple times, and your day becomes less rushed from the start. Maybe you turn off the music on the way to work and put on a success audio to grow yourself. Where can you make those little changes to make things happen? One little change can create a new habit and affect your goal for the positive.

Positive habits are non-negotiables for successful people. They know that having a routine of good, healthy habits is indispensable to their growth. How do successful people create and maintain good habits?

1. They make a decision to change something—either to create a new habit or eliminate a bad one. The decision has to be made first, then you can find the means to accomplish it. A new habit is never formed before the decision to create it is made.

2. They write down their non-negotiables. I have five habits I choose to do every day. They are my morning routine. They create a positive atmosphere right away in the morning to launch me into my day. When I miss my morning routine, I quickly lose steam, and it affects the productivity of my whole day.

3. Their coach knows about their non-negotiables. This holds them accountable to someone else and keeps them focused. It's easier to maintain when they let someone else in on their decision to change. They want to keep their word and not let their coach down. If they don't have a coach, they find an accountability partner to hold them to their plan.

4. They choose to win their day. These habits, the non-negotiables in their day, create a fire to push them on. The more they do them, the easier they become.

Work Ethic

Looking at your calendar can seem overwhelming. You may seemingly have so much on your plate that just looking at your weekly schedule can be a source of stress. You have work, appointments, kids' activities, service projects, possible meetups with friends, working out, and the list goes on.

I've learned to calm the stress by establishing the habit of planning my week on Sunday evenings and adding everything to my calendar. I schedule my workouts, phone appointments, and I include my husband's and kids' activities. Anything and everything goes on my calendar. But then I put aside the weekly view, and I make it a point to get through my list one day at a time. It breaks my week down into chunks that seem more doable. Even though there may be a plethora of events scheduled for the full week, when I look at it one day at a time, I see a doable day. It lessens my stress because I'm not thinking about all the other commitments throughout the rest of the week.

At night I look at the next day's plans. I set out my workout clothes and my day's outfit. This prepares me mentally so when I wake up, I've already formulated a plan. It sets me up to succeed at my morning routine. When I walk in the bathroom and see my workout clothes, I'm much more apt to get ready, get out there, and make things happen.

Along with planning our day-to-day, we need to actually get to work. Focus on doing at least one thing every day that will drive you closer to your goal. Have a plan to be productive throughout the day. Things don't happen without a plan. You need something set in place, written down, to hold you accountable to the task at hand. Your discipline is a daily decision.

Now here's the thing, keeping a calendar, and having a checklist of important things to do is great. But you need to ask yourself if it's just a checklist or if you are being intentional in doing the action pieces with excellence. Sometimes we can get in the habit of checking a box. We got it done! Yes! The problem is that we can get stuck in a rut if that's all we are doing. If we are doing things for the sole purpose of checking them off, then we are missing the mark. We put the list of habits or non-negotiables together in the first place because they are meant to get us to our desired end game. Whenever you do an action step, ask yourself if you're being intentional.

We need to ensure that our non-negotiables aren't just a checklist. I read for fifteen minutes today, check. I listened to a success audio, check. I got my long run in, check. We need to ask ourselves if we need to increase the rigor of any of our habits. Is reading fifteen minutes a day becoming too easy? Increase it to thirty minutes a day. What are you learning from the book? Are you reading for a purpose? Are you finding little nuggets that you can apply to your life? Are you taking the time to apply them to your life?

Sometimes we think we are doing all we can to prepare, but we don't realize that there is another level. Let's do an experiment that I learned at a leadership conference. I want you to raise your arm like you would to ask a question. Did you do it? Now... I want you to try and raise it a little higher. You could, couldn't you? You didn't raise it as high as you could have the first time.

Just like we don't immediately raise our arms as high as we could the first time, we have another level that we can push to when it comes to going after our goals. We can push more. We can do more. We can be more. We just need to be willing to stretch our arms up a little higher each time.

Dig Deep

We can't bring the past into it no matter what. We need to constantly be future focused. Those who focus on the past never move forward. Past experiences can be used to learn from, to fuel desire and focus, but they can't be dwelled on in a negative light.

If you miss a week of running, don't give up on your goal. It would be easy to quit when momentum is lost, but don't do it. Brush it off and move forward. I know this is easier said than done, and in order to actually be able to do that, you will need to sit down and formulate a plan for staying on the path toward your goal.

It's okay to fumble. What would you think of a football player who fumbles the ball and then stands there and watches the other team pick it up and run it to the endzone? It would look pretty silly. It would look like that player got out of the fight and lost hope. Don't follow up one mistake with the even bigger mistake of giving up. Fight back! Don't give up, keep going. Challenges will come. It's what we do with them that builds our character.

It would have been easy for me to look at my past finish times and say, "I don't think I can drop twenty-one minutes off my best time." If I focused on my past, I'd be stuck at that pace today. I had to declare that the past was in the past, and I am able to improve and have a great future. I'm able to lift my arm just a touch higher. When the going gets tough, drive your heels in, and dig deep. We don't truly know our potential until we're willing to dig a little deeper, go a little farther, or reach a little higher.

MENTAL DISCIPLINE

For me, training my brain was harder than the actual physical training. The mental toughness needed for marathon preparation weeds many people out, even before they start. It's a constant mind game—a constant battle.

Mental toughness is the will to keep fighting through seemingly impossible circumstances. If life were easy, we wouldn't have to learn how to get tough. There comes a point in a marathon—usually between miles eighteen and twenty—when runners hit what is known as "THE WALL." It is the breaking point where a runner experiences sudden fatigue or depleted energy. It's the point when many runners question whether they should drop out. Not all runners experience this phenomenon, but it is fairly common in the racing world.

This physical breaking point actually occurs because of depleted glycogen levels or when runners build up too much lactic acid in their muscles. But, no matter the cause, it often turns into a massive mental barrier in the race, which is why it is affectionately called "the wall."

I see "the wall" as a giant standing in our way. It's any obstacle that gets in the way of us continuing to pursue our goal. If we let it, "the wall" will take us out of our race. But how do we push past it?

Keep Going

Adversity is merely the enemy trying to distract us from our vision. Don't let distractions become louder than your vision or the coach speaking into your life. Adversity serves a purpose. You cannot have victory without adversity. It refines us, builds our character, and helps us become who we are meant to be.

"Consider it pure joy, my brothers and sisters, whenever you face trials of many kinds, because you know that the testing of your faith produces perseverance. Let perseverance finish its work so that you may be mature and complete, not lacking anything" (James 1:2-4).

Adversity is anything that tries to take you off course. It could be a major family tragedy, or it could be a small distraction, but either way, how you react to it will dictate if you stay there. If we fight through, and if we persevere, it will build up our character and mature us. Our experiences can give us new vision, new perspective, and clarity. They can develop us, define us, and create a warrior in us that will not be shaken and that will not give up until the job is complete. Each time we choose to persevere, we build our capacity for mental toughness and can more easily fight through the next obstacle.

Don't Look Back

You really can't change or overcome your past. It's just that—in the past. We could play the mind games of, "What if we did this," or, "What if we did that?" Would the outcome be different? Where would we be now? But, really, what's the point in questioning the "what ifs?" We cannot change what's already happened. Don't look back, rather focus on what lies ahead.

Did you hit "the wall?" See it as an obstacle that needs to be overcome, and overcome it. Don't focus on all the possible giants or situations that may arise. Don't worry about all the things that may eventually happen or come your way. Focus on the one giant staring back at you. These moments are defining moments in your life. Will you back down, or will you persevere? Your identity and your character become established through these defining moments.

Get Uncomfortable

Truth is, it is more comfortable to avoid "the wall," but you can't grow inside your comfort zone. Comfort is equal to settling. Being average is comfortable. Staying inside your comfort zone means you don't have to believe bigger. You can hide inside your shell and not be expected to execute at peak performance.

You can start coming up with reasons as to why success isn't such a big deal. However, once someone close to you breaks out of the ordinary grind and resolves to make a change, it can make you squirm because it forces you to question your own comfort.

Why not choose to do something now so you can truly live in peace knowing you have done something outside of yourself? In pursuit of a goal is the best place to be! It fuels your desires. It fuels your energy. It fuels purpose in your life.

Prepare Well

In order to not physically hit "the wall," runners need to make sure they are fueling correctly during their training. They need to prepare their bodies so they don't have to hit the wall at all. They need to figure out what they're going to use nutritionally—superstarches, gels, honey, electrolytes, and so on. They need to think about all these things so they don't lose that glycogen and so their levels stay balanced throughout the race.

The same goes with the mental game of life. How are you preparing mentally for today? How are you preparing to succeed? How are you preparing for whatever it is you're working toward? Are you listening to other people who are successful through audio, video, or live conferences? What about God's Word? Did you know it is filled with principles for success?

Are you reading? If you're not a reader, become one. Reading personal growth books is what actually changes you. You can take the written information and apply it. Audios are great, but they are more motivational. Reading can cut deep, it can help us self-reflect and see where we may be missing the mark or where we can become better. Focus, and get disciplined to be a reader. Who cares if you don't like it. Set the timer for ten minutes and start there. Force yourself to read something that's going to benefit you. Who knows? Maybe eventually you will grow to love reading—or at the least, you'll love the outcome of it.

Get out there and push past your wall! You don't have to be stuck behind your fears. You can rise to the challenge and bury your giant. I love what Bobby Knight, retired basketball coach of the legendary Hoosiers basketball team, says about preparation and getting past your "wall": "The key is not the will to win… everybody has that. It is the will to prepare to win that is important." The better you prepare, the easier it is to push past that wall and to the other side of victory.

Choose To Focus

Focus comes in the same package as a long-term vision. You need to know why you're doing what you're doing and bring those emotions to the forefront. Envision where you want to be. You can create desire with your mind.

My oldest son has developed mental toughness through gymnastics. He learned the keys to having a vision and seeing it through. As a level five gymnast, at age eight, he set the goal of winning the All-Around state title and placing top three at the regional championship. He did win his state meet. But then he even took it a step further, with more definiteness of purpose, and declared that he wanted a 67.0 all-around score at regionals.

He used the principles of affirmations and visualization, and wouldn't you know, his last event at regions was pommel horse, an event many male gymnasts struggle with. The meet was nearly over, and he was one of the last to compete. Commotion and noise surrounded him since many others had already finished and were finding their families. He could have succumbed to the distractions, but he locked in, completely focused, and smashed his routine. He hit a personal best score of 11.6, which brought him exactly to his goal of an all-around score of 67.0. Because of this, he also gained the title of regional champion, age eight, level five. There is power in focus.

Distraction is the enemy of focus. Anything that occupies your mind or time and takes you away from working toward your goal is a distraction to your dream. The only way to get rid of a bad habit is to replace it with a fresh one. Choose to fill old habits with new ones. Are you distracted by the television at night? Turn it off and open a book. Does your phone occupy your mind? Shut off the social media and turn on a success audio. Do you say "Yes" to everything and everyone? Choose to say "No" more frequently. If you say yes to one thing, you're automatically saying no to something else. Make sure your "Yes" is drawing you closer to your goal.

Be willing to put off distractions, or the "good," and reserve your precious focus for the "best." Don't get wrapped up in immediate gratification. Remember, goals take time, but achieving them is always worth it. In order to stay focused, put your long-term vision in front of you, and choose to do something every day toward that goal. Building consistency helps to create this focus. It keeps your dream in front of you.

There is power behind creating and maintaining a streak. You don't want to break it. Take, for example, my Scrabble-winning streak. As far as I know, I haven't lost a game—at least since I was too young to remember. I'm fairly proud of that statistic, though I get anxious every time I play to keep that streak going! Our eyes are glued to the TV screen when our favorite sports team is on a winning streak. Why? We love a streak! Why should it be any different when talking about our goals? Keep the focus and a streak of consistency.

Mental And Physical Intertwined

On a twenty-six mile training run, my hip popped out of alignment, and it was a difficult injury to overcome. I could actually tell the exact moment that it happened. I let fear creep in and try to steal my dream. I started thinking negatively and told myself that maybe I just wasn't capable of hitting my goal to qualify for Boston.

I chose to work toward overcoming my fears. Three weeks later, I nailed a twenty-seven mile training run. I did it to prove to myself that I can overcome that fear that had welled up inside. The fear was not of God. The fear was trying to paralyze me. This run forced me to push that worry aside.

119

I could have let my mind take me down this rabbit trail of negative thinking when my hip popped out. I could have chosen to be done and not do another long run before my race. Rather, I chose to discipline both my mind and my body and overcome that fear of injury or failure.

There are times when physically we do need to back off because of injury or overuse. We do need to be smart and listen to our bodies to tell us when enough is enough. But for me, I knew that I could push my body a little bit more without causing a serious injury, so I chose to do so.

My last training run proved I was disciplined to see my dream to completion. I could have chosen not to do it, and I may have been just fine, but I wanted to ensure that I had disciplined my flesh to the point I knew I could withstand whatever came my way.

My mind has everything to do with my work ethic. How I train my mind is as important as how much action I physically take. It takes major discipline to control your mind. Just like you would train your muscles to get stronger, you need to train your brain to be tougher. It takes time and effort. A negative brain can knock you out of the game.

Mental toughness is when you can find fuel in an empty tank. When you don't think you can continue, you find that extra burst of energy. The difference maker to be physically disciplined is in your mind.

EMOTIONAL DISCIPLINE

To burn means to be on fire or to be ablaze. When you burn something, it is consumed by the fire. When a goal becomes a burn, it means that no matter what, that specific goal becomes the most important thing. It is ingrained in us that it is going to happen no matter what we have to go through to obtain it. It "became a burn" means an all-consuming passion and desire toward the proposed goal. A fire is lit inside and goes ablaze, not stopping for anything until it has accomplished its purpose in its entirety. Emotional discipline means that you caught a burn for your goal and are willing to put aside your "feelings" and let your motivation or "burn" propel you forward.

Emotional Stability

There are ebbs and flows in all you do, and the point is to even the emotions out and find balance. When an obstacle comes, those who have high highs, who overcommit, or are high strung, will get down on themselves and move into a low low. They end up stopping their progress and doing nothing. We don't want that. We want an even-keeled consistency in all we do.

Do you know one of these people I'm talking about? I'm sure you do. The ones who are up one minute and down the next? You almost want to avoid them because you're not sure what you're going to get? We can't have those kind of extreme, swaying emotions when we are focused on hitting our goals.

A dog in the hunt doesn't know he has fleas. If you're focused and committed on your long-term vision, you don't have time to have high highs or low lows. You just keep going and continue to fight toward your goal. This is why it's vital that you know why you are doing what you are doing. This will bring emotion to the forefront and create the desire in your mind to go out there and do the work necessary to achieve your dream. Envision where you want to be, and soak up the emotion that is brought out through that.

Our children can teach us about emotional stability if we're willing to learn. The challenges they encounter become defining moments in their lives. Will they choose to rise above them? After his first nationals testing for men's gymnastics, at age ten, my oldest son taught me that disappointment is okay, but it's necessary to take "failure" and grow, not dwell on it.

He had his first tough meet and didn't hit any of his goals. He achieved Top 20 in the country for ten-year-old male gymnasts, which is a massive feat, but that wasn't his goal. His goal was to make National Team, which was Top 16.

Failure defines our character, and through this trial, I saw my ten-year-old son hold his head high, be proud of his accomplishments, and spark a fire inside himself, which drove him through the next season. Though I noticed disappointment written on his face after missing national team, he chose to use that setback to propel himself forward to the next level. He didn't make excuses or play the comparison game. He didn't blame anyone else. He didn't even play the "what if" and "if only" games that so many of us adults do.

We beat ourselves up over things we can't change rather than taking our failure as a learning experience and growing through it. Failure is actually necessary in order to succeed, but becoming defeated is one hundred percent optional. Failure defines our character. Do we let it take us out of the game and off course from what we are called to do? Or do we use it as fuel to drive us in the direction of our goal?

Just as my son had a choice to be emotionally disciplined, so do we when challenges arise. That gymnastics meet was a defining moment for him. He chose maturity. He chose strength. He chose growth. In your defining moments, what will you choose? Will you be a rollercoaster of emotion, or will you choose emotional stability? Will you turn and run from trials, or will you face them head on and let them build your character and mental toughness?

Excuses Are Fear-based

We talked some about excuses in Chapter Three and discovered that excuses boil down to three common fears: the fear of failure, the fear of what others think, and the fear of the unknown. Excuses play games with our emotions. Excuses get in the way of emotional discipline.

Here's a breakdown of some excuses, what they actually mean, and which fear they are playing into:

Excuse: *"No one's ever made it before."*
Actual meaning: "I have a fear of the unknown."

Excuse: *"My parents don't approve."*
Actual meaning: "I have a fear of what others think."

Excuse: *"What if it doesn't work out?"*
Actual meaning: "I have a fear of failure."

Who Cares What Others Think?

Getting emotionally tough means not caring what others think. We all love approval, and we can have a tendency to seek it out. However, when we are going after something that we know is important, the opinions of others cannot matter to us. When you are in the zone and working at accomplishing something, flack is going to come your way. Your family and your friends may not understand what you are doing or why it matters as much as it does. They may give you grief for not spending as much time with them, or they may tell you what you're doing won't work or that you're working too hard.

It's nice having your close buddies and family members on your side rooting for you, but they may not. What are you going to do if they don't back your goal? What are you going to do when someone tells you that you're wasting your time? Are you willing to buck up and stand your ground? Are you willing to keep pursuing what you know in your heart to be right and good?

The first time I ran the Twin Cities Marathon, I didn't notice hills at all. It didn't seem any harder than I thought it would be. The second time, however, everyone kept telling me how hilly and hard the course was, and I let it get to my head. I saw every single hill throughout that race, and it was taxing on my mindset. I let what others thought get the best of me.

Here's the thing. A lion is courageous and willing to break out of the pack. A lion is symbolic of strength and courage. Anyone who goes after his dream is a lion, fierce and mighty. Lions stand out. Lions command attention.

On the other hand, those who stay in the comfortable are more like sheep, mild and meek, not wanting to stand out. Sheep follow the leader without really asking questions. A sheep becomes highly agitated when it is separated from the flock. Sheep live in the comfortable. Sheep live to fit in. Sheep live in the routine.

A problem arises if we see ourselves as sheep when in all actuality we are lions. What do you see when you look in the mirror? Do you see the image of a lion, courageous and strong? Or do you still see yourself as a sheep, meek and powerless?

Don't let others dictate who you are and what you can or cannot accomplish. As a lion, you have a duty to break out of the pack and win. Read that last sentence again. Yes, I did say it is your DUTY. In doing so, you will inspire others to do the same. One person in pursuit of excellence automatically raises the standards and performance of everyone around them. Choose to be that person. Choose to be the lion. When you look in the mirror, who cares what others say you are? See the lion. You are the lion.

Hard Seasons

The season I worked full time, in addition to overnight shifts while homeschooling, was not a time I am anxious to re-live. While it was seemingly impossible to train for a marathon during that period, I had a dream that was bigger than my immediate difficulties. The bigger your "why," the easier the hard seasons become. They are never easy, but they don't have to beat us. Try to remember it is only a season. This too shall pass.

In the hard seasons, continue to take steps toward your goal. It may look a little different; you may not be able to run as hard as you want to, but keep going at some capacity. Choose to invest in yourself in the time you can find. Maybe you can only find a block of thirty minutes a day, but use that time! Choose to be productive in that thirty-minute window. It is even more important to be intentional about your actions if your time is working against you.

Don't pause "me" to take care of everyone else. Moms are the biggest culprits of this. They think they need to be all things to all people, but then they neglect filling themselves up. They are great caretakers of their kids, their husbands, and their friends, but they forget to be good caretakers of themselves. It is important to fill yourself up. If you run dry, then you no longer have anything to give.

When flying on an airplane, the flight attendant gets on the loudspeaker and goes through emergency procedures. When she gets to the part about the oxygen mask, she relays that you need to put your own mask on before helping anyone else, even your own children, with theirs. If you can't breathe, then you are no good to anyone else. It's vital to take time out for yourself no matter how busy you may be, so you are continually filled and have something to give others.

When you are in a hard season, if you keep walking in your purpose, God will multiply your time. You need to learn how to manage your time and resources well, and God will also multiply each of those things in your life.

No Quit Attitude

The main reason we need to push harder when we desire to quit is so that we can grow our mind muscles. We need to strengthen the mental toughness that lies within. When we work out, our response to stress or pain is rather immediate, so it's the perfect place to work on the mind muscles, to push ourselves to the next level. The physical aspect plays a part, but our mental strength can help push us through each mile, keep a constant pace, and hit a personal best.

When our body wants to slow down or quit, it's crucial for us to push past the pain and dig a little deeper. Our mental strength will do that for us. Don't be a slave to your mind. Learn to control it. We can train it just like we can train our muscles. It doesn't happen overnight because it's a never-ending process—we need to continually filter our thoughts. The more we do it, the easier it becomes, just as in the physical. The more miles we train, the easier it becomes, but we always need to be physically training, otherwise we'll go backward. If we stop, we regress.

How do we train our mind? How do we finally make the decision to overcome the negative? We have to pull the root, the source of our insecurities. We have to find the source of our insecurities or fears and deal with it head-on. Otherwise, it will continue to cycle, and we will never fully pull that toxic root from our lives.

We need to look deep inside and find the insecurities. Is it a wound from the past? Is it external from an empty childhood? A high school bully? Or is it internal, non-acceptance of ourselves? Are we nursing a character flaw? We need to embrace our weaknesses, and when we choose to accept them, they can, in turn, become fuel to drive us onward and upward. Make peace with your past, and then it's time to move on, stronger in character.

Olympic runner Desirce Linden knows what it feels like to want to quit. At the 2018 Boston Marathon, the thirty-degree chill, drenching rain, and 25 mph headwinds proved difficult for many, and she felt terrible near the beginning of the race. Rather than quitting, though, she chose to stay the course alongside Shalane Flanagan, a fellow Olympic runner.

"Early on, I was feeling horrible," Linden reminisced. "I gave [Shalane Flanagan] a tap and said, 'There's a really good chance I'm going to drop out today. If you need anything—block the wind, adjust the pace maybe—let me know.'"

She chose to stick it out and help a fellow elite runner. Flanagan even stopped to use the bathroom about halfway through the race, and Linden stopped to wait for her. That short rest helped give her a second wind and fresher legs, and she went on to win the race, becoming the first American woman to win in more than thirty years![6] What if she had decided to give in to her feelings and quit?

What was the difference maker? What gave Linden the edge? When all she wanted to do was quit, she chose to keep going, and she chose to take her eyes off herself and make it about someone else. She was determined to overcome the circumstances, push past her "wall," and finish strong. A no-quit attitude is a must!

FINAL STRETCH

This mental toughness mindset doesn't just happen overnight. It's a lifetime journey of learning and growing. It's taking each and every circumstance and being willing to grow from it. We strengthen our mental muscles just as we strengthen our physical muscles—by being disciplined to work them out daily.

God plants gifts and talents within each of us, and what we do with them is up to us. We glorify Him by developing these precious gifts to our fullest potential. What's at stake for you following these key areas of discipline? Your dream is what's at stake.

Is it possible that God plants these dreams and desires into our hearts with His plan in mind, a plan we don't see fully? What if us accomplishing our dreams is actually a key piece in God's plan for this world, and when we put our dreams on the back burner—or forget them all together—we are actually in disobedience to God's call on our lives?

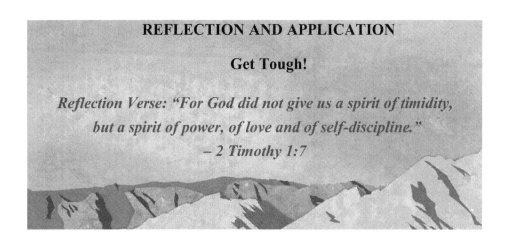

REFLECTION AND APPLICATION

Get Tough!

Reflection Verse: "For God did not give us a spirit of timidity, but a spirit of power, of love and of self-discipline."
– 2 Timothy 1:7

In Joshua 1:6-7, God instructed Joshua to listen to Moses and not deviate or turn to the left or right. Joshua needed to be completely focused on the task at hand and be willing not to become distracted. Distraction can slow you down in training or on race day. There are a plethora of things that can take you off course: the spectators, sounds, obstacles, wonderful sites, even your own thoughts. Distractions can turn out to be detours and take us off course if we let them. Choose to be mentally tough and tune out those distractions. Stay on course and don't deviate to the left or right no matter how pleasing the distraction may seem.

Reflection Questions:

1. Think back to a time when all odds were against you, and you wanted to quit. Did you? If so, what held you back? If not, what kept you going?

2. What's one thing you can do to become mentally tougher?

3. How can you stay more focused rather than turning to the right or left?

4. What "good" things have distracted you from pursuing God's "best" things for your life?

Further Reading:

- James 1:2-8
- Luke 10:19
- Philippians 4:13

Application: Create a Daily Habit Tracker

- Download the "Daily Habit" worksheet

Note: You can find the "Daily Habit" worksheet at www.redhotmindset.com/MOMresources

Chapter 8

Talk To Yourself

"I am, two of the most powerful words.
For what you put after them shapes your reality."
– Joel Osteen

The Book of James talks about the tongue being like the rudder on a ship. The rudder is the primary control force when it comes to steering the ship. When it is in working order, the rudder holds more power over the ship than even the wind has. But a passenger may not even see the significance of this small instrument.

The power of the rudder usually goes unseen, since it is hidden below the surface of the massive vessel. When the rudder turns, water strikes more forcibly on one side, and the ship turns toward the direction of less water pressure. If the rudder is off just slightly, it can mean a difference in destination by miles. James shares that just as a rudder is small, so is the tongue, but both have a monumental impact on the direction steered. Your life is steered by the thoughts you let control you and the words that you speak.

It is okay to talk to yourself! It's okay to tell yourself you're doing great. It's even okay to tell yourself that you are special and important. You can be your best encourager. It may look silly at first, but positive self-talk is significant in reprogramming your mind and keeping the negative out. In the same way, you can be your worst critic and biggest discourager. You can become your worst enemy just with the words you speak. Your words are a powerful force.

You always need to be on the lookout for what needs to be filtered out. A negative thought may seem harmless. It's no big deal, right? But if you let that negative thought creep in, soon you'll let in another and another, and they will infiltrate your mind like the plague—you won't even realize you were the one who allowed it. You can defeat yourself with your words before you even start. Don't do that. Words have a significant impact on your life. Be mindful about what is coming out of your mouth.

This will likely be the most impactful chapter for you, the reader. I know that when I learned the concept of self-talk, it revolutionized my life. This principle is probably one of the best kept secrets to living a joy-filled life, and I don't believe many have actually experienced what it can do for them. If applied, this principle WILL change your life.

WHAT IS SELF-TALK?

Self-talk, both negative and positive, is something people naturally do, yet they may not know its vast impact. Everyone talks to themselves, but what's important is whether they are talking nice or putting themselves down. What you say to yourself not only influences how you feel about yourself, but it also influences how you will respond in the circumstances that life brings your way. Self-talk can impact how others view us and how we interact with others. It has a huge bearing on our self-esteem, self-confidence, and self-worth. In essence, it affects how we see ourselves and the world around us.

Negative Self-Talk

Negative self-talk is anything you say to yourself that limits your belief in your own abilities. It is anything that makes you feel worse about yourself. In essence, it is disbelief in yourself and your potential, and it is toxic to your health, both figuratively and literally.

Negative self-talk can be disguised as *humility*, but it is actually extraordinarily toxic and quite the opposite of being humble. People don't want to be perceived as *full of themselves*, so they mask it by talking down about themselves instead. They call it their *inner critic*, which is a politically correct way to say *fault-finder*. Who wants to be around someone who is constantly finding faults about themselves or others? No one. We tend to avoid those people because we know they will pull us down into their negativity and self-pity. It's like being around Eeyore from Winnie the Pooh!

Negative self-talk creates a downward spiral effect rather than an uplifting one. Studies have shown that negative self-talk is linked to higher stress levels and lowered self-esteem. It can go as far as to lead one down the path toward depression or other mental and physical health problems. I know this from my own experiences, and I'll share about those a bit later in this chapter!

CUT OFF THE NEGATIVE

So how do we change things? It's easier said than done, but we have to cut off the negative. All negative flowing in and out of us. It's a constant battle we have to be willing to fight. We have to be willing to cut off any negative we try to place on ourselves, any negative coming at us from others, and we need to control our "I can't" statements. As we begin reprogramming our brain, the process does get easier, but it is never finished. It is a lifelong journey.

Don't Accept Negative From Yourself

We are our own worst critics. We get down on ourselves harder than we do anyone else, and we'd be shocked if we heard others talking about themselves the way we talk about ourselves. So why does it make it okay for us to talk that way to ourselves? Why do our thoughts tend to swing negative when we are alone or going through a hard place? We have to change that to move forward. We don't need to be controlled by our thoughts. Rather, we can choose to control them. We can learn the tools and skills to keep them from overpowering us and leading us down into a dark place. We can't let our thoughts paralyze us, rather we need to let them carry us in a positive direction!

I believe my depression story began when I was in high school. The thing is, if you knew me back then, you would have had no idea. I was popular enough, athletic, and socially adept. I loved being surrounded by others and being the center of attention. I was involved in a plethora of extra-curricular and church activities. I was even the baseball mom, aka the manager. However, when I was alone, negative emotions overcame me, and I'd find myself slowly seeping into the darkness of hopelessness and despair. I couldn't pinpoint where any of those thoughts and emotions were coming from. I just knew that they were real and scary.

I was able to keep things at bay through high school and into college. I thought it was normal, or at least that's what I told myself. When I approached my mom, she told me I just had some blues, and it would go away. To her credit, she had no idea what I was truly going through within myself because she saw the outside me, the one I portrayed to others, the bubbly, happy-go-lucky teenager and young adult. So that's what I thought it was, just the blues—normal.

I had huge aspirations and lofty goals, so I figured it must be the blues like my mom said. I couldn't have been dealing with depression when my life looked like it was headed in such a positive and successful direction. That just couldn't happen to someone like me. I had a strong faith, and sometimes I think I hid myself behind that.

The culmination occurred during my junior year of college. Once again, I had so much going for me. Dozens of friends, boys chasing after me, intramural sports, and a spot on the coveted newspaper staff. But there was a hole deep inside that I just couldn't seem to fill no matter how many friends I had or social gatherings I attended.

I felt like I was losing control of myself and my circumstances. I dealt with some eating disorders, over-exercising, and eventually started cutting myself. These were the ways I could find control. Again, no one would have seen any of that coming. They saw me as this positive, friendly college student ready to take on New York and the largest broadcast network! I only had one friend who asked me about the cuts just above my knees, and I just shrugged it off as an accident, a mere scrape. She never questioned me again.

Right before Christmas Break, I found myself at my lowest point, thoughts of taking my own life actually flooded my mind, something I knew I would never do, yet it pulled on me. The mind is a powerful thing, and I had programmed it to think so negatively about myself that the thought of living in hopelessness discouraged me. I was tired of feeling so miserable, so helpless. It was at that point that I knew I needed help, and thank God I reached out.

I called the mental health services on campus, and they told me they don't usually take on new clients before a break. I folded. The tears flowed, and I had a breakdown right there on the phone. The lady on the other end of the receiver quickly and wisely said to me, "You need to come in right now." And that was that. They proceeded to give me the support I needed. I went to counseling and was put on medication. I had to get it out of my head that medication or help was bad. I felt like I should have been able to deal with all these thoughts and emotions on my own, but I quickly realized that it had become so much larger than myself. Over time, it had overpowered me and caused me incredible shame.

I was ashamed to talk about it. I didn't want anyone to know what I was dealing with because I was afraid of what they would think. Can I tell you something? What others think doesn't matter. The medication helped. It stabilized my emotions so I could work on the skills necessary to combat the negative that seeped into my soul. It had such a stronghold on me, but I found out that I could retrain my brain and dig myself out of the darkness that I felt.

It wasn't easy. It was hard, so hard. I began a journey of reading self-development books. Some of the books were recommended by my psychologist, and some I found on my own at the bookstore. When I graduated, I began a mentor-led leadership training program, and I continued the journey of self-discovery.

I began to reprogram my thoughts, and I slowly came out of the depression and overturned the negative with positive. When I learned this concept of self-talk and truly applied it to my life, I was able to come out of that very deep and dark depression and eliminate all medication! It wasn't overnight, it was a slow process, but it was a dramatic difference when I chose to stop medication. I have never gone back. I have my days when I feel off. I have those times when I find myself trying to pull back toward that negative and spiral downward, but I have now learned the skills and have the tools to negate those feelings before they overtake me. I now can get myself back on track when the negative tries to steal my joy.

Once you gain a positive mental attitude (PMA), it is easier to remain positive in tough circumstances because you have learned the tricks to combat the negative trying to creep inside.

Don't Accept Negative From Others

Words can build up, and they can destroy. You also need to be careful what you listen to, or more specifically, who you listen to. Mark 4:24 says, "Be careful what you hear because what you hear will be multiplied unto you." Words have power when you speak them, and words have power when you hear them. What you listen to or watch is what will consume your mind. That goes back to why association is so important. Just as you can't unsee something, you also can't unhear it.

I think back to some of the music I listened to in high school, and it all had catchy tunes, but when I dial in and actually listen to the lyrics, they are not positive at all. I've heard a few of them lately and thought to myself, "I can't believe I listened to that!" There is subliminal messaging in all forms of entertainment, whether we think there is or not. Even movies I used to watch as a kid that I thought were harmless are full of language or sexual innuendos that I wouldn't want my kids hearing.

Negative people equals negative thoughts and a negative outlook. Positive people equals positive thoughts and a positive outlook. Period. Where do you want to be on the spectrum? Do you remember the Sunday School song, "Be careful little eyes what you see... Be careful little ears what you hear?" Very true and powerful lyrics. We need to be constantly aware of what content we are filling our minds with.

Think back to childhood for a moment. I bet you can remember someone who told you that you could do anything you wanted to if you just set your mind to it and encouraged you to push harder. Think about that. Who was that person in your life? Was it a teacher, a relative, a friend? What did you want to do because of it? How did they make you feel? How did they encourage you? When you were around them, they empowered you to be better. Their words uplifted you, and you felt better about yourself when you parted ways.

From ages seven to fourteen, Emily Blunt stuttered. Her junior high teacher encouraged her to try out for a school play and suggested that she try her hand at different accents and character voices. She was a dream maker in Blunt's life. She wasn't willing to give up on her and believed she could overcome her circumstances.

Wouldn't you know, that by her late teens, Blunt had lost her stutter. She is well-known for her roles in *The Devil Wears Prada* and *The Girl on the Train* movies, and she became a Golden Globe Award recipient. Her junior high teacher believed in her enough for her to eventually believe in herself.[1]

Now think back again to your childhood, and I bet you can remember someone who discouraged you by saying your dream was dumb or impossible or unrealistic. How did that person make you feel? Did you start doubting yourself and your dream? Did it put a blockade in your way of achievement? Both of those people had great power in your life. Whom did you choose to listen to?

A friend of mine has a son who was a gymnast several years before my oldest started on the team, but she told me a story of an incident he had with one of his coaches and how it affected him years later. He was a solid gymnast and took first in his age group at regionals. He then switched gyms, and that new coach told him not to expect to be regional champion again that coming year.

This may not seem like a huge deal, but it had such an impact on his young mind. He lost his love for gymnastics and eventually decided to quit. Now, I'm not sure that was all due to this particular coach, but this young man went on to write a high school paper about the impact his coach's words had on him. Those words from his coach still have effects on him today. Our words, once they are spoken, cannot be taken back.

Why is it that as a child we shoot for the moon and as adults we disbelieve? We've programmed ourselves to think that what we once longed to do is now impossible. We've listened to the naysayers too long. We've let average people dictate what our lives should look like. The problem is that we believed the lies instead of listening to the voice of truth. We were all born with seeds of greatness in us, but too many of us leave them to die deep inside instead of nurturing them to grow and flourish.

Stop Saying "I Can't"

One phrase I do not allow in my house is, "I can't." I don't like it because it focuses on the negative. Simply reframing this phrase can make a huge impact on your life. I once heard someone say that rather than "I can't," they phrase it as "How can I?" What a great spin on it! Rather than immediately denying your abilities, you try to find a solution as to how you can make it work.

For example, imagine you had a list of things to get done, and you didn't accomplish the whole list. You might think, or say, "I can't believe I didn't get it all done today." The wording of that automatically makes you feel like a failure. But if you rephrase it and said, "How can I make sure I get that done?" you're being proactive and constructive with your words. You're empowering yourself to accomplish your necessary tasks without shaming yourself. You're looking for a solution rather than focusing on the problem.

When I hear my boys say, "I can't," I immediately ask them to rephrase their words to, "How can I?" Then we work through the situation together and find constructive solutions. However, if I ask them to do this exercise, I need to be willing to uphold it myself. I lead by my example.

Just because you can't doesn't mean God won't! Your dream may seem impossible in the physical, but if something was placed on your heart, and you feel like it is a call on your life, nothing is impossible with God. Sometimes a big dream means we need to get out of our own way and realize it is impossible – on our own strength.

If you're a believer, you serve a big God who wants to use you to do big things. With Him the impossible becomes possible. He loves to use weak people to do great things. All we need to be willing to do is believe and trust that what's placed on our hearts is important. I'm sure that's why God uses unlikely people to do extraordinary things.

138

Maybe that's why we're supposed to have childlike faith. God knows that a child will do something without disbelief at least once because he doesn't know any better. Childlike faith is innocent and vulnerable.

Positive Self-Talk

Positive self-talk is affirming in nature. It is encouraging and uplifting. It reaffirms the good in who you are and helps you to believe in the good qualities you possess. It builds confidence in your gifts and talents and helps you to see that you actually can have a purpose and make a difference in this world. Positive self-talk is all about "I am" statements. I am worthy. I am strong. I am courageous. I am a good mom. I am full of self-confidence. I am quick on my feet. The list goes on.

We hear our own voice more than anyone else's. We hear it all day long, every minute of the day. It's one thing that we can't get away from. Why would we want to fill our words with such negative filth about who we say we are?

Think back to my husband's love of Corvettes and how he began seeing them everywhere all because he had them on his mind. What you talk about is what you'll notice the most. If you're speaking positively, you'll see the silver lining in circumstances. You'll begin to see more opportunities, and you'll be able to make the best in every situation. Through positive self-talk, you'll start seeing solutions rather than problems. It is said that positive people find a solution for every problem, and negative people find a problem for every solution. Which one do you choose to be?

Why Does It Work?

What you choose to focus on is what you will begin to believe. The mind is a wildly powerful tool. When you dwell on a specific statement, essentially self-talk, your brain will eventually reprogram itself to believe what you are speaking over yourself. It will, in essence, paint a new picture in the control center of your body and give you an entirely new outcome.

One of my all-time favorite books is *What to Say When You Talk to Yourself* by Shad Helmstetter, Ph.D. I encourage you to pick up a copy and read it. It was life changing for me and helped me understand the science behind my words. After reading it, I was able to reprogram some self-sabotaging statements I had spoken over myself in the past.

These were the statements that had eventually led me down the rabbit hole into a depressive state, and I was immersed in that dark place for years, unaware of what I was doing to myself. Know that there is hope for you if you are experiencing any of those dark thoughts right now!

Our minds are like a computer. We need to program them because they calibrate our expectations, and our expectations calibrate how effective or successful we will be. In the computer world, the acronym GIGO stands for "Garbage In, Garbage Out," and just as a programmer uses that to filter systems, we need to filter our minds. We bring a thought in, decipher if it is positive or negative, and the negative ones have to go, they're garbage. GIGO can also stand for "Good In, Good Out." If our brain is like a computer, it will produce exactly what we program it to, whether it's good or garbage. A computer is only as good as the data you give it. The mind is only as good as the thoughts you allow it to keep. What we put in is what will come out. Our minds will perform to the expectations we set. We need to be able to speak our vision over ourselves. When we program our minds right, it raises the level to which we can perform and creates a better us.

Here's our practical application. Look down the road to the best version of yourself that you can imagine. Do you see him or her? Start speaking that person's (your future self's) character over yourself so you can grow into the person you were meant to be all along. Is it a confident and bold personality you wish to have? Speak, "I am bold and confident." Are you wanting to be financially free? Speak, "I live in abundance, lacking nothing." Do you want to run your first marathon or ultra-race? Imagine yourself at the finish line. Imagine yourself as that person right now. Choose to use your words wisely for your good and not negatively against you.

PROACTIVELY SPEAK THE POSITIVE

Words produce faith—either good or bad—depending on the words. The words you speak either work for you or against you. They are either words of faith or words of doubt. Faith comes from God. Doubt comes from the devil. Fear will activate Satan and faith will activate God. Listen to the voice of truth. Say, "I am a warrior of the king; I am a princess, and I deserve to reach my goals." Once you know who you are and, more importantly, whose you are, you will begin to realize you were made for greatness!

Overcome Negative With Positive

How do you overcome a negative thought? With a positive word. You cannot think negative while speaking positive. It's so simple, and it works. Don't believe me? Try it! The next time a negative thought pops into your head, say something positive out loud. You couldn't think about that negative thought while speaking, could you? Words are so powerful. Think about this. God created the heavens and the earth by *speaking* them into existence. If God created the world with words, they must be fundamental in our lives.

It was so important for me to have positive self-talk throughout my training. The only way to negate a negative thought is to speak a positive word. When negative started creeping in my mind as I was training and running the race, I would speak against it. I talked out loud, and I didn't care if people around me thought I was crazy (In all actuality, I was probably helping them out as well).

My goal was too important to lose to negative thinking. When my legs hurt, I'd tell myself they were light, quick, and ready. When my breathing changed, I'd tell myself I had the lung capacity and endurance to finish strong. When I felt like quitting, I told myself I was a winner, and winners don't quit. It's normal for me to speak things out loud like, "I'm awesome!" "I got this!" "I'm strong!" I need to convince myself that I am capable, and so do you.

When I'm training for races, I dwell on my past successes, not on my past failures. I can learn from my failures on how to train differently or

141

fuel differently, but if I dwell on them, I won't move on from them. They'll always be there, in the back of my mind, on every training run, and it will become a self-fulfilling prophecy. If I dwell on my failures, I will feel like a failure. If I dwell on my successes, it will lead to more successes.

I keep a solid training log with my mileage, time of day, type of workout, how I fuel, which shoes I wear, and so on. In that training log, I also record how my workouts go each day. This helps me to see if maybe I was having an off day or if certain times of the day are better or certain fuel in my body helps me perform better than others. But, one thing I do every single time is write something positive about that workout down, even if the workout didn't go the way I wanted. It helps me to view my workouts and training in a positive light. If I wasn't running my normal paces and just felt off, maybe I'd write in there that I was proud of myself for getting out there and hitting the pavement.

Allow yourself to win by being your best encourager. It may seem egotistical or boastful, but it's not. You were designed to succeed and win. We weren't designed to live a life of quiet desperation. Negative thoughts are only controlled with positive words. Capture your thoughts!

The Power Of "I Am"

- I am worthy.
- I am confident.
- I am courageous.
- I am qualified.
- I am strong.
- I am confident.
- I am a butt kicker.

"I am." These are two powerful words that can change your whole perspective. These words create for you the image of who you are. They are personal, and you can decide what you put after them. Do you choose to speak life over yourself? Do you choose to see yourself in a positive light and imagine who you believe you can be?

Choose A Mantra… Or Two

A mantra is something that you can speak when you are feeling tired, negative, or defeated. Think of it as a little pick-me-up despite the circumstances. Some of my mantras on race day include:

- "I'm worthy, and it's my time."
- "I'm strong, and my feet are swift."
- "I've trained for this moment."
- "The hills make me stronger."

You talk to yourself more than you talk to anybody else. You are always in your own head. How do we overcome the negative and doubt that creeps up in our minds? The only way to eliminate a negative thought is with positive words. So don't be embarrassed! Talk to yourself! The other runners around you will appreciate the encouraging words as well.

Thoughts – Spoken Words:

My legs hurt – My legs are strong

My lungs burn – My oxygen supply is endless

Maybe it's not worth it – My dream is always worth it

I can't do it – I can do hard things!

I still have 5 miles – I'm 21 miles in! I've got this.

More Positive Self-Talk Running Mantras:

I trained for this moment.

I will not let this course beat me.

I can dig deep a little longer.

I can push a little more.

I have what it takes.

My legs are light, and my feet are quick

Words Are Seeds

Words are similar to seeds. By speaking them aloud, they are planted in our subconscious minds, and they take on a life of their own; they take root, grow, and produce fruit of the same kind. We can nurture and cultivate them with more positive words. Our words are also the water that gives life to the fruit we produce.

My oldest son has his words working for him. He has already learned the power of positive. He will tell you he is awesome and strong and smart. He will also tell you that he's going to the 2028 Olympics in Los Angeles and winning the gold medal in men's gymnastics. He fully believes he is meant to do that. And guess what? I'm not going to tell him any differently because who am I to tell him his dream is too big?

Our problem as adults is that our dreams are too small. We forgot how to dream in the midst of our "rite of passage" into adulthood. My son has a colossal dream, and he'll tell you he can do all things through Christ who strengthens him. He wants a greater influence so he can help others. I'm so proud of how his mind works. He's a living, breathing example of the confidence you can have when you believe and speak the positive. Allow your subconscious mind to go there!

What is one of the best ways to start training your brain to recognize the negative? Say it out loud. How does it sound when you say it out loud? Does it sound harsh? Is it condescending in nature? Would you readily make those same comments about and to a friend? Would you say those things to your children? Sometimes that's the best measure you can have. Ask yourself honestly if you would say those same derogatory thoughts to a friend. Ninety-nine percent of the time your answer would be, "Absolutely not! That's not appropriate!" Well, then, why do you think it is appropriate for you to say those things about yourself?

DIFFERENT TYPES OF SELF-TALK

Self-talk comes in many different varieties. It starts by simply not speaking any negative, and then moves into speaking goals as if they already are, speaking who you truly are and who you want to become, and speaking life over others.

Don't Speak Negative

We need a "bouncer" at the door of our minds, chucking anything negative out and allowing positive to seep in. 2 Corinthians 10:5 says, "We take captive every thought to make it obedient to Christ." Isn't that like having a bouncer at our mind's door? We are conscious about what is coming in, we immediately take it captive, and then we decide what to do with it. Is it negative? Throw it out! Is it positive? Then choose to speak it.

What you focus on, you will have. Have you seen the people who are constantly sick? What do they focus on? What do they post about on social media? Their focus is constantly on being sick. They are training their subconscious to be sick. We don't have to fool ourselves. If we are feeling sick or struggling financially or hating our job or finishing a terrible workout, we don't have to pretend everything is amazing. That's not the point. The point is to not stay in a negative state because we can choose our attitude even if we can't choose our circumstances.

We don't have to claim sickness or destitution or unhappiness. We may feel it, and our circumstances may seem that way, but we can choose to ensure our words do not affirm it. If I'm feeling sick and someone tells me I look it I will answer that I am overcoming. I'm not denying how I feel, but I'm also not opening the door to the negative in my mind.

What you focus on, you will have. If you say, "I'm broke, I never have any money," you will keep yourself from ever having money. Rather, say, "My God shall supply all my needs according to his glorious riches." Don't say, "I'm so tired I can hardly function." Rather, say, "I will soar on wings like eagles. I will run and not grow weary." Choose to be driven by gratitude rather than fear. When we are grateful, we don't have time to be negative or look at the negative circumstances surrounding us. Gratefulness exudes positivity.

Speak Goals As If They Already Are

Once you have a handle on not speaking negatively, the next step is to learn how to get your words working for you. This is extremely important. Do not speak what you have, speak what you want. By speaking what you want, not what you have, you will start to subconsciously make changes in your lifestyle to achieve those goals.

The same is true for the negative. If you speak negative or against your goal, then that's what you'll get. You'll say things like, "I'll never lose those ten pounds." "It's impossible to make more money." "I'm going to be broke forever." "I'll never be able to retire." "I'm always tired." "I can't get organized." "Nothing good ever happens to me." "I don't have what it takes." "I can't do it." "I'll never get out of this mess." The list goes on and on. With those words, you've trained your brain to make sure those things happen. They negate what you're trying to accomplish.

Speak Who You Truly Are Or Want To Become

We are our toughest critics. All the negative that rolls around in our minds about how we won't measure up—we would never think to say those things to other people. We'd be nicer and more uplifting. So why is it so hard to be that way toward ourselves?

When I'm struggling during my training, I think about what I'd say to a runner whom I was coaching at that very moment and try to apply that same approach to myself. It's usually easier to coach someone else because it's not as personal, but if we use the same advice on ourselves that we give to others, we will see progress. So take a minute to determine a couple of things. Who are you? Who do you want to become?

Speak Life Over Others

When we're focused on others and how we can be a blessing to them, we don't have time to dwell on our shortcomings. Putting our eyes on someone else takes the limelight off ourselves. It keeps us from wallowing in our own issues or negative thoughts. We automatically feel better about ourselves after reaching out and giving to someone in need.

Here's the thing. Most likely others are speaking negatively about themselves. They are focusing on the bad and their failures more than they are on the positives and their strengths. They're thinking about how they messed up at work or were late to an appointment or couldn't get anything right. They haven't read this book... yet! When we share a smile or an encouraging word with someone else, they are blessed. It's amazing what one positive word can do to change a person's entire day. We never know what's going on in someone else's mind, and our words can play a major role in how they internalize their feelings about themselves.

Experiment With Apples

Dr. Masaru Emoto is well-known for his groundbreaking discovery that water is actually connected to our individual and collective consciousness. He tried to create crystals in water, and when he played music around the frozen chunk of water, crystals in the form of snowflakes formed in the ice.

He claims it has to do with the vibrations and resonance. Everything in the world is made up of energy, so everything has vibration—even our words and thoughts. We are made up of 70 percent water, so the energy and vibrations can, in fact, affect us as well.[2]

Have you heard of the famous apple experiment? It's rather neat, and I'd been meaning to do it with my boys at home to see firsthand how it works, so we finally did! Here's what you do. You take an apple and cut it in half. You put one half enclosed in one jar and another half in another jar. Separate them from each other, and start speaking to them. We are made up of 70 percent water, and apples are made of 86 percent water, so it's a close comparison.

Think about all the negative things you think or say to yourself. Start saying those things to the negative apple. Start saying what you want it to do. "You are a rotten apple." "You are not worthy." "Why don't you just rot?" "You mean nothing to me."

On the other hand, think about all the positive things you think or say to yourself. Start saying those things to the second apple. "You are beautiful." "You are worthy." "You are forever ripe." "You are luscious and flavorful."

We did this with both apples and also with rice. With the rice, we placed one cup of water and one cup of rice into three jars. We labeled one jar as "good", one as "bad", and one as "ignore." We spoke to each jar every day, sometimes multiple times a day.

At the end of the thirty days, the rice in the "good" jar was still near the top of the water line. The rice in the "bad" jar had sunk a bit lower, and the rice in the "ignore" jar sunk even lower. The "good" apple was still fresh looking and didn't have any noticeable mold on it, but the "bad" apple was rotting and definitely didn't look edible.

Here are some things we learned from doing the apple and rice experiments:

- Words build us up. Words can tear us down.

- Words energize. Words can draw depression.

- Words bring courage. Words can produce fear.

- Words heal. Words can usher in sickness.

- Words bring life. Words can bring death.

How we talk about ourselves affects how we think about ourselves and what we produce. If words are powerful enough to affect a small piece of fruit, how much more can they affect us? Words actually MATTER!!!

FINAL STRETCH

The rudder controls the direction of the ship, just as your tongue controls the direction of your life. One single, small spark can set a forest on fire. In the same way, your life can go up in flames just by the words that you speak over yourself. The mouth is a powerful force. Choose to create a habit of positive self-talk. You frame up your world with your words.

REFLECTION AND APPLICATION

Positive Self-Talk

Reflection Verse: "Finally, brothers, whatever is true, whatever is noble, whatever is right, whatever is pure, whatever is lovely, whatever is admirable—if anything is excellent or praiseworthy —think about such things."
— Philippians 4:8

Words are extremely powerful. Think about this. God created the heavens and the earth by speaking them into existence. If God created the world with words, they must be important. With words, Jesus healed the sick (Matthew 8:3). With words, Jesus calmed the storm (Luke 8:22). With words, Jesus cursed the fig tree, and it died (Mark 11:12). Words can build up, and words can destroy. Choose your words wisely. From the heart, the mouth speaks. The Bible is filled with verses specific to the tongue. Here are just a few:

- "Does not the ear test words as the tongue tastes food?" (Job 12:11)
- "My lips will not say anything wicked, and my tongue will not utter lies." (Job 27:4)
- "Set a guard over my mouth, Lord; keep watch over the door of my lips." (Psalm 141:3)
- "The words of the reckless pierce like swords, but the tongue of the wise brings healing." (Proverbs 12:18)

- "The soothing tongue is a tree of life, but a perverse tongue crushes the spirit." (Proverbs 15:4)
- "The tongue has the power of life and death, and those who love it will eat its fruit." (Proverbs 18:21)
- "Those who guard their mouths and their tongues keep from calamity." (Proverbs 21:23)
- "She speaks with wisdom, and faithful instruction is on her tongue." (Proverbs 31:26)

Reflection Questions:

1. What have you allowed to enter into your mind through entertainment that you may need to give up in order to keep a positive mind?
2. What is one negative thing you say to yourself multiple times a day? How can you switch that to be a positive affirmation?
3. What are three "I am" statements that you want to implement into your daily affirmations? Who do you want to say you are?

Further Reading:

- James 3:1-12
- Ephesians 4:29-32
- Matthew 15:11
- Psalm 19:14
- Mark 11:12-25

Application: Make an affirmation card—index card with 3-5 positive affirmations on it. Read it out loud 3x a day (i.e. when you wake up, at lunch, before bed).

Here are some examples:

- "I am strong and courageous, for my God is with me wherever I go." (Joshua 1:9)
- "I am a good communicator, and people want to hear what I have to say."
- "People like me, and I make friends everywhere I go."
- "I am worthy of success."
- "I am full of self-confidence and bold in my convictions."
- "I am fit and able to hit a personal best race."
- "I am capable of running (insert race here) well."

Chapter 9

Crush Your Goals

"Watch your thoughts; they become words.
Watch your words; they become actions.
Watch your actions; they become habits.
Watch your habits; they become character.
Watch your character; it becomes your destiny."

– Lao Tzu

You can train as hard as you want, but you will never fully be prepared for race day. You can control the controllables—your training and your attitude—but how can you completely prepare for the unexpected? You can study the terrain, but there's always going to be that bump in the road that you didn't see on paper. It may get simpler with each race, and you may gain more clarity each time, but the journey to the finish line is never the same.

Even though you can't entirely prepare for the unexpected, you also can't wait for perfect conditions to start—you just have to trust the process and get to work! As I was in the midst of my training, I signed up for a half marathon, a 15k, and a couple of 5ks. I figured it would help me gauge if my training was working or if I needed to tweak anything specific along the way.

I ran the Iron Girl Half Marathon in Clearwater, Florida, while on a family vacation. My goal was to have a personal best, and I not only achieved that, but I also placed 9th overall. I had never been in a position of placing in a race, so I was ecstatic. I beat my half marathon time by more than two minutes, and it was at that point that I truly believed that if

I just kept doing what I was doing, I would accomplish what I set out to do.

After a few more races of different lengths with similar results—crushing my personal bests and placing in my age group—I started to realize I was stronger, faster, and more determined than I ever thought possible.

I'm not telling you my stats to toot my horn. I relay them to show you the power of mentality in training. When I finally qualified for Boston at the 2015 Grandma's Marathon, the only thing that had changed was how I mentally prepared. In turn, it revealed that I wasn't working to my best potential. I had more to give.

A few years after I qualified for my first Boston Marathon, I had a nagging urge to use this mentality to drive me there a second time. I wanted to test my method once again to ensure that the principles in this book work, and that I had something to offer. I have had three main goals in this process:

- Step 1: Qualify for the Boston Marathon for the first time.
- Step 2: Duplicate a Boston qualifying time (BQ) in another race.
- Step 3: Write a book that will inspire others to follow their dreams.

Step One - Do It For The First Time

Qualify for the Boston Marathon.

Achieving my time goal at the 2015 Grandma's Marathon was step one. Check. Done. I fought through the pain and hit a pretty significant dream in my life. I know I wouldn't have had the passion or drive to finish strong like I had if it weren't for the months of mental training leading up to race day. I also knew, though, that we could call it an anomaly since I had only done it once. Could I do the same thing again? Could I change the goal to be more challenging and still accomplish it?

When we accomplish a goal, it feels great, it's a job well done. We should be thrilled, but we shouldn't just stop there. We need to re-evaluate and stretch ourselves by setting a new goal. We should be continually climbing to new heights.

After hitting a goal for the first time, we can downplay it and think, "I just got lucky," or "This is a fluke." But, here's the thing. If you do it once, you can do it again. Once you prove to yourself that you are able, you now move into an "I can" attitude. You know you are good enough. You know you are strong enough. You now have the keys to setting out and accomplishing any goal.

Once you know you can do it, you move into the next step - choosing to be willing to do it again. You have to ask yourself the question, "Will I?" When you find out you "can", you have to decide you "will." Now it's a matter of willpower. You know you can put in the work, and you know you can discipline yourself enough. Now you need to decide if you are willing.

Step Two - Do It Again

I wanted to ensure it wasn't an anomaly and that it actually was my mental training that gave me the edge. I hired a coach to help me with the accountability of the physical training, and I got to work on the mental side. My goal this time was to hit a sub-three hour and thirty minute time, a three hour and twenty-five minute marathon to be exact.

After you decide what it is you really want to work toward, it's important for you to make a game plan, find someone willing to speak into your life, and to trust the game plan and see it through.

The 2018 St. George Marathon in Utah was the race I chose to prove my method. 3 a.m. on race day came fast! I hit the shuttle by 4 a.m. to make the scenic drive through Snow Canyon State Park to the starting line.

It rained during the full three hours while we anxiously awaited the gun start. Ironically, it was only the third time in the St. George race history that it rained. The race began a half hour late, still raining, cloudy, and dark. I didn't have control of the weather. I didn't have control of the late start. I didn't have control of the fact that my preferred playlist didn't work in the altitude. All of these things were out of my control.

You need to learn to control the controllables and forget about what you can't control.

I could only control two things—my actions and my attitude. My action was the training I had put in the last four months, physically and mentally. It was my choice to have an attitude of fear or an attitude of faith. Two words played over and over in my mind throughout the race: GRIT and FIGHT. I could do this.

Negative crept in.

No matter how strong you are, negative will come. It's what you do with it that defines you. Don't let the negative take you out.

I chose to speak to my negative. I had two main mantras throughout: "I am worthy," and "It's my time." I broke down my miles into chunks. At mile seven I said, "I'm already more than a fourth of the way there." At mile eighteen I said, "I only have two hard miles left," knowing I had a huge buffer in time. At mile twenty, I broke it down to two 5ks left. The last six miles was all heart. A marathoner needs to dig deep and discover strength in that last stretch.

It's important to break down your larger dream with smaller goals because it's the long term vision that drives you, but the smaller goals keep you consistent and pressing on.

When I reached the corral leading to the finish, I saw that clock with the bright red numbers flashing back at me... 3:18:28 as I passed under it. What a sweet victory! I broke down in tears knowing I had not only hit my goal, but I had crushed it. I beat my main goal by almost seven minutes and hit another BQ by almost seventeen minutes. It was surreal!

At any point, I could have chosen to give up or slow down. I could have been okay with running the race in three hours and thirty-three minutes, good enough for a solid BQ. But I didn't. I wanted to push my limits and see what I was capable of. I'm proud of myself for holding strong physically and mentally. I'm proud of myself for doing hard things.

I'm proud of myself for not making excuses. I'm proud of myself for overpowering my negative thoughts with positive words.

This is the power of desire and determination. In any goal you set out to do, you have to be willing to get mentally tough and stay strong throughout the course.

I had said I wanted a fifteen minute buffer for a qualifying time, which is why I chose to train for a three hour and twenty-five minute race, but last minute, after more than seven thousand qualifiers were turned away from running the Boston Marathon for 2019, race officials dropped qualifying times for all age groups by five minutes for 2020. For the 2019 Boston Marathon, qualifiers had to average four and a half minutes quicker than their specified qualifying time. So mentally, that was stuck in my head.

Also, in 2018, I jumped up an age group. My BQ was supposed to be a three hour and forty-minute marathon. With the announcement of qualifying times dropping, the new time I had to beat was three hours and thirty-five minutes, which is what it was back in 2015 on my first go around. I knew I'd have to hit at least a three hour and thirty minute time to ensure a spot at the Boston Marathon in 2020. Mentally, I wanted that fifteen minute buffer, and I focused on that so much, that I still got it with my finish time!

This is the power of visualization. It's important not only to have the goal, but also to burn the desired outcome into your mind so you can truly see yourself with whatever it is you are striving for.

There is power in our mind. When we do it once, we can do it again. We can choose to keep pushing. Our mind is our limit. Winning can become a habit, and it's a great habit to form. Achieving goals is a worthwhile habit to form in your life. It's up to you to develop the mental strength to push past the obstacles and continually hit your goals. Choose to focus. Choose mental strength. Choose to win.

Step Three - Leave A Legacy

Finally, I wanted to share what I've learned by writing a book that will inspire others to go after their dreams.

As I'm writing this very book, I'm fulfilling a childhood dream. Since as young as I can remember, I've longed to be a published author. I knew one day I would affect others through the written language. Doubt and fear crept in on my journey to complete this manuscript. I was stopped in my tracks so many times with thoughts of unworthiness, but I knew it was because there's meaning and significance in it.

I don't want to hit my expiration date with anything left inside. I want to know I put it all out there and did my best to walk in my calling and pursue my passion. I want to know that I did all I was capable of so I can hear, "Well done, good and faithful servant," when my time to meet my Maker comes.

My story needed to be heard, and so does yours. We need more dreamers. We need more people to stand up and say yes to the call to be extraordinary. Say "no" to average and "yes" to your calling. The time is now. See what you're made of and become who you were created to be.

Your goals aren't just about you. They're about what you can bring to the world. What legacy will you leave for your family and those surrounding you?

NOW IT'S YOUR TURN

Are you ready to turn your dreams into a reality? Are you beginning to feel worthy of achievement? Can you picture yourself at your finish line? I want so badly for you to dream a dream larger than yourself and to work at it until you get there! You are worthy, and it's your time. If this is a journey you want to embark on, the steps are simple:

- **Step One: Develop Your Dream**

- **Step Two: Create a Written Game Plan**

- **Step Three: Get To Work And Crush Your Goals**

FINAL STRETCH

It starts with a dream. What's nagging on your heart? What have you always wanted to do? See it. Let the image of you succeeding burn in your mind. Post pictures that motivate you toward it. Don't just visualize, but also make a game plan. How are you going to achieve your goal? Be determined to the end. Don't let obstacles take you out. Let them make you that much better. Grow a burning passion for your dream until it becomes a need. Trust your game plan. If you have a coach, trust your coach. Don't worry about how it won't come to fruition, have faith that it will. Stay tough mentally. Don't sway. Be focused. Use positive self-talk to empower yourself and keep negative out. Talk to your mountain, and tell it to move! Lastly, go out there and be a goal crusher! We were made to achieve more. We are only truly living when we are following our dreams. Don't stifle the greatness inside of you. Don't be labeled as a person that people say was full of potential. Let it out and see what you are capable of. I think it will surprise you! You are a winner, just run YOUR race!

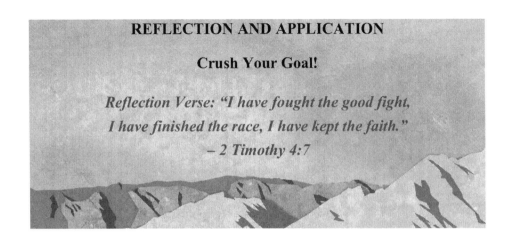

REFLECTION AND APPLICATION

Crush Your Goal!

Reflection Verse: "I have fought the good fight, I have finished the race, I have kept the faith."
— 2 Timothy 4:7

Has God placed something on your heart to complete? I've always been good at starting—but that's usually where it ends. I've learned, however, that when God places a task on my heart, I need to see it to completion because it now becomes an obedience factor. If I decide to stop before completion, I'm being disobedient to my call, and, in turn, telling God I don't trust HIS plan or HIM! If God calls us to do something, it's going to be hard. It's going to stretch us, and we probably won't be able to do it on our own. However, He calls us to it for a reason, and we will change in the process.

Remember, He doesn't call the equipped, He equips the called—we just have to answer that call. He WILL give us more than we can handle so we HAVE to trust and rely on Him. His ways are not our ways, and His thoughts are not our thoughts. They are so much more expansive than we can imagine. However, we also will never know the goodness or the blessings if we don't latch onto His plan and see our calling to completion. Everything changes when we decide to finish. Don't give in. Finish strong. It's always worth it. "I press on toward the goal to win the prize for which God has called me heavenward in Christ Jesus" (Philippians 3:14).

Reflection Questions:

1. What is nagging you on the inside? What are you feeling called to step out in faith and do?

2. Are you willing to see your dream to completion no matter what it takes?

3. Have you had an experience where you know God called you to do something and you didn't do it? What was the result?

4. Have you had an experience where you know God called you to do something and you did do it? How did you feel?

Further Reading:

*   Proverbs 16:3
*   James 1:5
*   John 10:10

Application: READ THE NEXT STEPS SECTION

*   Download the "Red Hot Affirmations" PDFs
    *   Personal Growth
    *   Spiritual Growth
    *   Running Mantras

Note: You can find the "Red Hot Affirmations" PDFs at
www.redhotmindset.com/MOMresources

Notes

Chapter 1

1. *I Can Only Imagine*. Directed by Andrew Erwin, and Jon Erwin. Santa Monica: Lionsgate, 2018.

Chapter 2

1. Runners World. "Everything You Need to Know About Iliotibial Band Syndrome." Published on April 3, 2018. https://www.runnersworld.com/health-injuries/a19576110/iliotibial-band-syndrome/

Chapter 3

1. Wikipedia Contributors. "J. K. Rowling," Wikipedia, The Free Encyclopedia. Accessed on April 21, 2019. https://en.wikipedia.org/w/index.php?title=J._K._Rowling&oldid=900175487
2. *Merriam-Webster, s.v.* "Dream," accessed on April 21, 2019. https://www.merriam-webster.com/dictionary/dream
3. Ibid.
4. Forbes. "Permission To Fail: Leadership Lessons From Babe Ruth's Bat." Published on June 17, 2014. https://www.forbes.com/sites/robasghar/2014/06/17/permission-to-fail-leadership-lessons-from-babe-ruths-bat/#670f958644b2
5. Makers. "Happy Birthday, Oprah! 5 Things You Didn't Know About the Media Mogul and Philanthropist." Published on January 29, 2015. https://www.makers.com/blog/happy-birthday-

oprah-5-things-you-didnt-know-about-media-mogul-and-philanthropist

6. Newsweek. "Michael Jordan Didn't Make Varsity—At First." Published on November 17, 2015. https://www.newsweek.com/missing-cut-382954

7. Thought Catalogue. "35 Famous People Who Were Painfully Rejected Before Making It Big." Published on October 14, 2013. https://thoughtcatalog.com/rachel-hodin/2013/10/35-famous-people-who-were-painfully-rejected-before-making-it-big/

8. Ibid.

9. Ibid.

Chapter 4

1. *Oxford Dictionaries, s.v.* "Vision," accessed on April 21, 2019. https://en.oxforddictionaries.com/definition/vision

2. *Oxford Dictionaries, s.v.* "Wisdom," accessed on April 21, 2019. https://en.oxforddictionaries.com/definition/wisdom

3. *The Bible, King James Version.* Public Domain. (Proverbs 29:18)

4. Dr. Caroline Leaf, "Dr. Leaf's Research." Accessed on June 13, 2019. https://drleaf.com/about/dr-leafs-research/

5. Lindsey Hoffman. "Celebrities Whose Vision Boards Came True." Published on February 26, 2015. https://www.doseofbliss.com/celebrities-whose-vision-boards-came-true/

6. News Observer. "Retirement, the future of Duke and Kobe Bryant: A one-on-one interview with Coach K." Published on February 13, 2018. https://www.newsobserver.com/sports/college/acc/duke/duke-now/article199904324.html

7. Lindsey Hoffman. "Celebrities Whose Vision Boards Came True." Published on February 26, 2015.

https://www.doseofbliss.com/celebrities-whose-vision-boards-came-true/

8. Seth Muse. "An Unbreakable Vision of the Future." Accessed on April 21, 2019. http://www.sethmuse.com/unbreakable-vision/

Chapter 5

1. Napoleon Hill, *Think and Grow Rich* (New York: Random House Publishing Group, 1960), Chapter 2.
2. Thomas A. Edison Quotes. BrainyQuote.com, BrainyMedia Inc, 2019. Accessed June 13, 2019. https://www.brainyquote.com/quotes/thomas_a_edison_109004
3. Mom's on the Run. "About." Accessed on April 21, 2019. https://www.momsontherun.com/about.html
4. Uncommon Influence. "One Degree Off Course." Accessed on June 13, 2019. http://www.uncommoninfluence.com/one-degree-off-course/

Chapter 6

1. *Merriam-Webster, s.v.* "Distraction," accessed on April 21, 2019. https://www.merriam-webster.com/dictionary/distraction
2. New York Post. "Americans Check Their Phones 80 Times a Day: Study." Published on November 8, 2017. https://nypost.com/2017/11/08/americans-check-their-phones-80-times-a-day-study/
3. Hacker Noon. "How Much Time Do People Spend on Their Mobile Phones in 2017?" Published on May 9, 2017. https://hackernoon.com/how-much-time-do-people-spend-on-their-mobile-phones-in-2017-e5f90a0b10a6
4. Nielsen. "Time Flies: U.S. Adults Now Spend Nearly Half a Day Interacting with Media." Published on July 31, 2018.

https://www.nielsen.com/us/en/insights/news/2018/time-flies-us-adults-now-spend-nearly-half-a-day-interacting-with-media.html

Chapter 7

1. Wikipedia Contributors. "Glenn Cunningham (athlete)," Wikipedia, The Free Encyclopedia. Accessed on April 21, 2019. https://en.wikipedia.org/w/index.php?title=Glenn_Cunningham_(athlete)&oldid=896604140

2. Maxwell, John. *Make Today Count: The Secret of Your Success is Determined by Your Daily Agenda.* New York: Center Street, 2004.

3. *Oxford Dictionaries, s.v.* "Resilience," accessed on April 21, 2019, https://en.oxforddictionaries.com/definition/resilience

4. *Oxford Dictionaries, s.v.* "Determination," accessed on April 21, 2019, https://en.oxforddictionaries.com/definition/determination

5. Nielsen. "Time Flies: U.S. Adults Now Spend Nearly Half a Day Interacting with Media." Published on July 31, 2018. https://www.nielsen.com/us/en/insights/news/2018/time-flies-us-adults-now-spend-nearly-half-a-day-interacting-with-media.html

6. Runners World. "The Science Behind How Sportsmanship Helped Desiree Linden Win Boston." Published on April 19, 2018. https://www.runnersworld.com/training/a19862759/sportsmanship-desiree-linden-boston-marathon/

Chapter 8

1. The Muse. "9 Famous People Who Will Inspire You to Never Give Up." Accessed on April 21, 2019.

https://www.themuse.com/advice/9-famous-people-who-will-inspire-you-to-never-give-up

2. Emoto, Marsaru. "Interview with Dr. Masaru Emoto about the magic of Water (Rice Experiment)." Interview by Newtide TV. Published on August 3, 2008.
https://www.youtube.com/watch?v=ujQAk9EM3xg

Next Steps

Use your imagination and discover your dreams in this FREE course that coincides with Chapters 1-3 of *Mind Over Marathon*! Check it out at www.redhotmindset.com/MOMresources

I would love nothing more than to help you develop your dreams and take them to the finish line! I can be your coach as you create your unique game plan and get into the action mode pursuing your passions. Head on over to www.redhotmindset.com/courses to learn how you can work with me, and join me today in the race of our lives!!

Share your "race" story with me! Is there something that jumped out at you while reading? What principles would you like to implement first from this book? I'd love to hear from you! Please send me a DM on Instagram @redhotmindset or share your thoughts on social with the hashtag #MindOverMarathon and tag me in your post!

Join the discussion in our FREE Mind Over Marathon online community! You can share your thoughts and takeaways from the book with fellow dreamers as well as get into the action mode to bring those dreams to fruition! It's a place where accountability and community are organically created. Join here:
www.facebook.com/groups/mindovermarathon

Leave a Review!

If you enjoyed this book, please take a moment to leave a review.

Your review helps in so many ways!

Readers choose books based on recommendations. Leaving an Amazon or Goodreads review is like telling your friends how much you enjoyed *Mind Over Marathon*. After 20 reviews, Amazon starts to promote the book in the "you might like" lists. After 50 reviews, Amazon might promote *Mind Over Marathon* by email. This would be HUGE for *Mind Over Marathon*.

Your review means the world to me! Thank you for reading and reviewing at www.amazon.com/author/gabecox.

I hope you have gained much value from this book! Thank you for reading!

~ Gabe Cox

Acknowledgments

Thank you first to my husband, Josh, who encourages me to pursue my running and writing goals and has been my rock throughout the entire process.

To my boys, Ethan, Micah, and Gavin, who not only inspire me daily but always let me out the door for my runs knowing I need that time to rejuvenate and reflect. They have taught me how to dream huge and stretch me to be a better version of myself every day.

To my mentors, Matt and Alana Grotewold, who have raised me up as a leader and spent hours teaching me success and foundational life principles.

To Ami Wilson, my friend and confidant. Our friendship has withstood the test of time, and I love that she has never been willing to leave me where I'm at. She's always stretching me to be better and dream larger.

To Kristen Genet, one of my best running friends who spent endless hours in the beginning of this journey reading my manuscript and asking more questions. She's been a thrill to coach as she worked toward achieving her own Boston qualification time, which enabled her to run in the 2019 Boston Marathon.

To my running coach, Antonio Vega, for pushing me to the next level and helping me tap into my hidden potential.

To my parents, Warren and Sandy Wicklund, who sacrificed so much for me as I was growing up. They always backed me on my dreams and encouraged me to continue to pursue them. They still do today!

I want to give special recognition to the specific people who have helped me create a beautiful book.

Thank you to Jody Henning of Jody The Girl, LLC for a perfect cover design and additional graphics: https://jodythegirl.wixsite.com

To Emily Deady for professionally editing my book: http://www.editing.emilydeady.com

To Kitty Turner, Founder and CEO of Daily House Publishing, for being my consultant and rock throughout the entire book launch process: https://dailyhouse.media

And, thank you mostly to my Lord and Savior Jesus Christ. All glory and honor goes to Him who redeemed me and gave me the burning passion and gift to write and impact others through my experiences.

About The Author

Gabe Cox is an author, speaker, and coach who resides in Andover, Minn., with her husband and three boys. She first qualified for the Boston Marathon in 2015, which allowed her to run in the 2016 race. She has since qualified again and will be participating in the 2020 Boston Marathon. She used the principles outlined in this book to achieve a Boston qualifying time and continues to use them as she strives toward new goals in running and life. She is a mental training coach and RRCA certified running coach who is passionate about pushing others toward their goals and inspiring them to dream huge. Her mission is to help others overcome their mental barriers so they can run their best race, live their best lives, and achieve their dreams.

Connect with Gabe Cox in your favorite location:

Website: www.redhotmindset.com

YouTube: www.youtube.com/RedHotMindset

Facebook: www.facebook.com/redhotmindset

Instagram: https://www.instagram.com/redhotmindset/

Linkedin: https://www.linkedin.com/in/redhotmindset/

Snail Mail: P.O. Box 11, Champlin, MN 55316

At the finish of the 2015 Grandma's Marathon where I hit my first Boston qualification time, and I was able to put on a shirt for the first time that symbolized my dream.

My family is the reason I choose to go after my dreams, so I can model for them what it means to succeed.

The 2016 Boston Marathon was a special race for me, as it brought back the memories of what it took to fight for my spot at the start line.

Made in the USA
Monee, IL
02 January 2020

19785343R00109